JAMESTOWN  EDUCATION

TIMED READINGS

25 Two-Part Lessons
with Questions for
Building Reading Speed and Comprehension

BOOK SIX

Edward Spargo

Mc Graw Hill **Glencoe McGraw-Hill**

New York, New York   Columbus, Ohio   Chicago, Illinois   Peoria, Illinois   Woodland Hills, California

JAMESTOWN ⛵ EDUCATION

Glencoe/McGraw-Hill 𝒳

A Division of The **McGraw·Hill** Companies

Timed Readings Plus, Book Six, Level I

ISBN :   0-0-89061-908-5

Send all Inquiries to:
Glencoe/McGraw-Hill
8787 Orion Place
Columbus, OH 4324

11 12   045   10 09 08

CONTENTS

TO THE INSTRUCTOR

Overview

Timed Readings Plus is designed to develop both reading speed and comprehension. A timed selection in each lesson focuses on improving reading rate. A nontimed selection—the "plus" selection—follows the timed selection. The nontimed selection concentrates on building mastery in critical areas of comprehension.

The 10 books in the series span reading levels 4–13, with one book at each level. Readability of the selections was assessed by using the Fry Readability Scale. Each book contains 25 lessons; each lesson is divided into Parts A and B.

Part A includes the timed selection followed by 10 multiple-choice questions: 5 fact questions and 5 thought questions. The timed selection is 400 words long and contains subject matter that is factual, nonfiction, and textbook-like. Because everyone—regardless of level—reads a 400-word passage, the steps for the timed selection can be concurrent for everyone.

Part B includes the nontimed selection, which is more narrative than the timed selection. The length of the selection varies depending on the subject matter, which relates to the content of the timed selection. The nontimed selection is followed by five comprehension questions that address the following major comprehension skills: recognizing words in context, distinguishing fact from opinion, keeping events in order, making correct inferences, and understanding main ideas.

Getting Started

Begin by assigning students to a level. Students should start with a book that is one level below his or her current reading level. If a student's reading level is not known, a suitable starting point would be one or two levels below the student's present grade in school.

Teaching a Lesson: Part A

Work in each lesson begins with the timed selection in Part A. If you wish to have all the students in the class read a selection at the same time, you can coordinate the timing using the following method. Give students the signal to preview. Allow 15 seconds for this. Have students begin reading the selection at the same time. After one minute has passed, write on the chalkboard the time that has elapsed. Update the time at 10-second intervals (1:00, 1:10, 1:20, etc.). Tell the students to copy down the last time shown on the chalkboard when they finish reading. They should then record this reading time in the space designated after the selection.

If students keep track of their own reading times, have them write the times at which they start and finish reading on a separate piece of paper and then figure and record their reading time as above.

Students should now answer the ten questions that follow the Part A selection. Responses are recorded by putting an X in the box next to the student's choice of answer. Correct responses to eight or more questions indicates satisfactory comprehension and recall.

Teaching a Lesson: Part B

When students have finished Part A, they can move on to read the Part B selection. Although brief, these selections deliver all the content needed to attack the range of comprehension questions that follow.

Students next answer the comprehension questions that follow the Part B selection. Directions for answering the questions are provided with each question. Correct responses require deliberation and discrimination.

Correcting and Scoring Answers

Using the Answer Key at the back of the book, students self-score their responses to the questions in Parts A and B. Incorrect answers should be circled and the correct answer should be marked. The number of correct answers for Part A and for Part B, and the total correct answers should be tallied on the final page of the lesson.

Using the Graphs

Reading times are plotted on the Reading Rate graph at the back of the book. The legend on the graph automatically converts reading times to words-per-minute rates. Comprehension totals are plotted on the Comprehension Scores graph. Plotting automatically converts the raw scores to a comprehension percentage based on four points per correct answer.

Diagnosis and Evaluation

The Comprehension Skills Profile graph at the back of the book tracks student responses to the Part B comprehension questions. For each incorrect response, students should mark an X in the corresponding box on the graph. A column of Xs rising above other columns indicates a specific comprehension weakness. Using the profile, you can assess trends in student performance and suggest remedial work if necessary.

A student who has reached a peak in reading speed (with satisfactory comprehension) is ready to advance to the next book in the series. Before moving on to the next book, students should be encouraged to maintain their speed and comprehension on a number of lessons in order to consolidate their achievement.

How to Use This Book

Getting Started

Study Part A: Reading Faster and Better. Read and learn the steps to follow and the techniques to use to help you read more quickly and more efficiently.

Study Part B: Mastering Reading Comprehension. Learn what the five categories of comprehension are all about. Knowing what kind of comprehension response is expected from you and how to achieve that response will help you better comprehend all you read.

Working a Lesson

Find the Starting Lesson. Locate the timed selection in Part A of the lesson that you are going to read. Wait for your instructor's signal to preview the selection. Your instructor will allow you 15 seconds for previewing.

Read the Part A Selection. When your instructor gives you the signal, begin reading. Read at a faster-than-normal speed. Read carefully so that you will be able to answer questions about what you have read.

Record Your Reading Time. When you finish reading, look at the blackboard and note your reading time. Write this time at the bottom of the page on the line labeled Reading Time.

Answer the Part A Questions. Answer the 10 questions that follow the selection. There are 5 fact questions and 5 thought questions. Choose the best answer to each question and put an X in that box.

Read the Part B Selection. This passage is less textbook-like and more story-like than the timed selection. Read well enough so that you can answer the questions that follow.

Answer the Part B Questions. These questions are different from traditional multiple-choice questions. In answering these questions, you must make three choices for each question. Instructions for answering each category of question are given. There are 15 responses for you to record.

Correct Your Answers. Use the Answer Key at the back of the book. For the Part A questions, circle any wrong answers and put an X in the box you should have marked. For the Part B questions, circle the wrong answer and write the correct letter or number next to it.

Scoring Your Work

Total Your Correct Answers. Count your correct answers for Part A and for Part B. Record those numbers on the appropriate lines at the end of the lesson. Then add these two scores to determine your total correct answers. Record that number on the appropriate line.

Plotting Your Progress

Plot Your Reading Time. Refer to the Reading Rate graph on page 116. On the vertical line that represents your lesson, put an X at the point where it intersects your reading time, shown along the left-hand side. The right-hand side of the graph will reveal your words-per-minute reading speed. Your instructor will review this graph from time to time to evaluate your progress.

Plot Your Comprehension Scores. Record your comprehension scores on the graph on page 117. On the vertical line that represents your lesson, put an X at the point where it intersects your total correct answers, shown along the left-hand side. The right-hand side of the graph will reveal your comprehension percentage. Your instructor will want to review this graph, too. Your achievement, as shown on both graphs, will determine your readiness to move on to higher and more challenging levels.

Plot Your Comprehension Skills. You will find the Comprehension Skills Profile on page 118. It is used to record your wrong answers only for the Part B questions. The five categories of questions are listed along the bottom. There are five columns of boxes, one column for each question. For every wrong answer put an X in a box for that question. Your instructor will use this graph to detect any comprehension problems you may be experiencing.

PART A: READING FASTER AND BETTER

Step 1: Preview

When you read, do you start in with the first word, or do you look over the whole selection for a moment? Good readers preview the selection first. This helps to make them good—and fast—readers. Here are the steps to follow when previewing the timed selection in Part A of each unit.

1. Read the Title. Titles are designed not only to announce the subject, but also to make the reader think. What can you learn from the title? What thoughts does it bring to mind? What do you already know about this subject?

2. Read the First Sentence. Read the first two sentences if they are short. The opening sentence is the writer's opportunity to greet the reader. Some writers announce what they hope to tell you in the selection. Some writers tell you why they are writing. Other writers just try to get your attention.

3. Read the Last Sentence. Read the final two sentences if they are short. The closing sentence is the writer's last chance to talk to you. Some writers repeat the main idea once more. Some writers draw a conclusion—this is what they have been leading up to. Other writers summarize their thoughts; they tie all the facts together.

4. Scan the Selection. Glance through the selection quickly to see what else you can pick up. Look for anything that can help you read the selection. Are there names, dates, or numbers? If so, you may have to read more slowly. Is the selection informative—containing a lot of facts, or is it conversational—an informal discussion with the reader?

Step 2: Read for Meaning

When you read, do you just see words? Are you so occupied reading words that you sometimes fail to get the meaning? Good readers see beyond the words—they seek the meaning. This makes them faster readers.

1. Build Concentration. You cannot read with understanding if you are not concentrating. When you discover that your thoughts are straying, correct the situation right away. Avoid distractions and distracting situations. Keep the preview information in mind. This will help to focus your attention on the selection.

2. Read in Thought Groups. A reader should strive to see words in meaningful combinations. If you see only a word at a time (called word-by-word reading), your comprehension suffers along with your speed.

3. Question the Writer. To sustain the pace you have set for yourself, and to maintain a high level of concentration and comprehension, question the writer as you read. Ask yourself such questions as, "What does this mean? How can I use this information?"

Step 3: Grasp Paragraph Sense

The paragraph is the basic unit of meaning. If you can discover quickly and understand the main point of each paragraph, you can comprehend the writer's message. Good readers know how to find the main ideas quickly. This helps to make them faster readers.

1. Find the Topic Sentence. The topic sentence, which contains the main idea, is often the first sentence of a paragraph. It is followed by sentences that support, develop, or explain the main idea. Sometimes a topic sentence comes at the end of a paragraph. When it does, the supporting details come first, building the base for the topic sentence. Some paragraphs do not have a topic sentence; all of the sentences combine to create a meaningful idea.

2. Understand Paragraph Structure. Every well-written paragraph has a purpose. The purpose may be to inform, define, explain, illustrate, and so on. The purpose should always relate to the main idea and expand on it. As you read each paragraph, see how the body of the paragraph is used to tell you more about the main idea.

Step 4: Organize Facts

When you read, do you tend to see a lot of facts without any apparent connection or relationship? Understanding how the facts all fit together to deliver the writer's message is, after all, the reason for reading. Good readers organize facts as they read. This helps them to read rapidly and well.

1. Discover the Writer's Plan. Every writer has a plan or outline to follow. If you can discover the writer's method of organization, you have a key to understanding the message. Sometimes the writer gives you obvious signals. The statement, "There are three reasons . . ." should prompt you to look for a listing of the three items. Other less obvious signal words such as *moreover, otherwise,* and *consequently* tell you the direction the writer is taking in delivering a message.

2. Relate as You Read. As you read the selection, keep the information learned during the preview in mind. See how the writer is attempting to piece together a meaningful message. As you discover the relationship among the ideas, the message comes through quickly and clearly.

Part B: Mastering Reading Comprehension

Recognizing Words in Context

Always check to see if the words around a new word—its context—can give you some clue to its meaning. A word generally appears in a context related to its meaning. If the words *soil* and *seeds* appear in an article about gardens, for example, you can assume they are related to the topic of gardens.

Suppose you are unsure of the meaning of the word *expired* in the following paragraph:

> Vera wanted to take a book out, but her library card had expired.
> She had to borrow mine because she didn't have time to renew hers.

You could begin to figure out the meaning of *expired* by asking yourself, "What could have happened to Vera's library card that would make her have to borrow someone else's card?" You might realize that if she had to renew her card, it must have come to an end or run out. This would lead you to conclude that the word *expired* must mean to come to an end or run out. You would be right. The context suggested the meaning to you.

Context can also affect the meaning of a word you know. The word *key*, for instance, has many meanings. There are musical keys, door keys, and keys to solving a mystery. The context in which key occurs will tell you which meaning is right.

Sometimes a hard word will be explained by the words that immediately follow it. The word *grave* in the following sentence might give you trouble:

> He looked grave; there wasn't a trace of a smile on his lips.

You can figure out that the second part of the sentence explains the word *grave:* "wasn't a trace of a smile" indicates a serious look, so grave must mean serious.

The subject of a sentence and your knowledge about that subject might also help you determine the meaning of an unknown word. Try to decide the meaning of the word *revive* in the following sentence:

> Sunshine and water will revive those drooping plants.

The sentence is about giving plants light and water. You may know that plants need light and water to be healthy. If you know that drooping plants are not healthy, you can figure out that revive means to bring back to health.

Distinguishing Fact from Opinion

Every day you are called upon to sort out fact and opinion. When a friend says she saw Mel Gibson's greatest movie last night, she is giving you her opinion. When she says she saw Mel Gibson's latest movie, she may be stating a fact. The fact can be proved—you can check to confirm or verify that the movie is indeed Mel Gibson's most recent film. The opinion can be disputed—ask around and others may not agree about the film's unqualified greatness. Because much of what you read and hear contains both facts and opinions, you need to be able to tell them apart. You need the skill of distinguishing fact from opinion.

Facts are statements that can be proved true. The proof must be objective and verifiable. You must be able to check for yourself to confirm a fact.

Look at the following facts. Notice that they can be checked for accuracy and confirmed. Suggested sources for verification appear in parentheses.

- In 1998 Bill Clinton was President of the United States. (Consult newspapers, news broadcasts, election results, etc.)

- Earth revolves around the Sun. (Look it up in encyclopedias or astrological journals; ask knowledgeable people.)

- Dogs walk on four legs. (See for yourself.)

Opinions are statements that cannot be proved true. There is no objective evidence you can consult to check the truthfulness of an opinion. Unlike facts, opinions express personal beliefs or judgments. Opinions reveal how someone feels about a subject, not the facts about that subject. You might agree or disagree with someone's opinion, but you cannot prove it right or wrong.

Look at the following opinions. Reasons for classification as opinions appear in parentheses.

- Bill Clinton was born to be a president. (You cannot prove this by referring to birth records. There is no evidence to support this belief.)

- Intelligent life exists on other planets in our solar system. (There is no proof of this. It may be proved true some day, but for now it is just an educated guess—not a fact.)

- Dog is man's best friend. (This is not a fact; your best friend might not be a dog.)

As you read, be aware that facts and opinions are frequently mixed together. The following passage contains both facts and opinions:

> The new 2000 Cruising Yacht offers lots of real-life interior room. It features a luxuriant aft cabin, not some dim "cave." The galley comes

equipped with a full-size refrigerator and freezer. And this spacious galley has room to spare. The heads (there are two) have separate showers. The fit and finish are beyond equal and the performance is responsive and outstanding.

Did you detect that the third and fifth sentences state facts and that the rest of the sentences express opinions? Both facts and opinions are useful to you as a reader. But to evaluate what you read and to read intelligently, you need to know the difference between them.

Keeping Events in Order

Writers organize details in a pattern. They present information in a certain order. Recognizing how writers organize—and understanding that organization—can help you improve your comprehension.

When details are arranged in the precise order in which they occurred, a writer is using a chronological (or time) pattern. A writer may, however, change this order. The story may "flash back" to past events that affected the present. The story may "flash forward" to show the results of present events. The writer may move back and forth between past, present, and future to help you see the importance of events.

Making Correct Inferences

Much of what you read suggests more than it says. Writers do not always state outright what they want you to know. Frequently, they omit information that underlies the statements they make. They may assume that you already know it. They may want you to make the effort to figure out the implied information. To get the most out of what you read, you must come to an understanding about unstated information. You can do this through inference. From what is stated, you make inferences about what is not.

You make many inferences every day. Imagine, for example, that you are visiting a friend's house for the first time. You see a bag of dog food. You infer (make an inference) that the family has a dog. On another day you overhear a conversation. You catch the names of two actors and the words *scene, dialogue,* and *directing.* You infer that the people are discussing a movie or play.

In these situations and others like them, you infer unstated information from what you observe or read. Readers who cannot make inferences cannot see beyond the obvious. For the careful reader, facts are just the beginning. Facts stimulate your mind to think beyond them—to make an inference about what is meant but not stated.

The following passage is about Charles Dickens. As you read it, see how many inferences you can make.

Charles Dickens visited the United States in 1867. Wherever he went, the reception was the same. The night before, crowds arrived and lined up before the door. By morning the streets were campgrounds, with men, women, and children sitting or sleeping on blankets. Hustlers got ten times the price of a ticket. Once inside, audiences were surprised to hear their favorite Dickens characters speak with an English accent. After 76 readings Dickens boarded a ship for England. When his fellow passengers asked him to read, he said he'd rather be put in irons!

Did you notice that many inferences may be drawn from the passage? Dickens attracted huge crowds. From that fact you can infer that he was popular. His English accent surprised audiences. You can infer that many didn't know he was English. Hustlers got high prices for tickets. This suggests that "scalping" tickets is not new. Dickens refused to read on the ship. You can infer that he was exhausted and tired of reading aloud to audiences. Those are some obvious inferences that can be made from the passage. More subtle ones can also be made; however, if you see the obvious ones, you understand how inferences are made.

Be careful about the inferences you make. One set of facts may suggest several inferences. Not all of them will be correct; some will be faulty inferences. The correct inference is supported by enough evidence to make it more likely than other inferences.

Understanding Main Ideas

The main idea tells who or what is the subject of the paragraph or passage. The main idea is the most important idea, the idea that provides purpose and direction. The rest of the paragraph or passage explains, develops, or supports the main idea. Without a main idea, there would only be a collection of unconnected thoughts. It would be like a handle and a bowl without the "idea cup," or bread and meat without the "idea sandwich."

In the following passage, the main idea is printed in italics. As you read, observe how the other sentences develop or explain the main idea.

Typhoon Chris hit with full fury today on the central coast of Japan. Heavy rain from the storm flooded the area. High waves carried many homes into the sea. People now fear that the heavy rains will cause mudslides in the central part of the country. The number of people killed by the storm may climb past the 200 mark by Saturday.

In this paragraph, the main idea statement appears first. It is followed by sentences that explain, support, or give details. Sometimes the main idea appears at the end of a paragraph. Writers often construct that type of paragraph when their purpose is to persuade or convince. Readers may be more open to a new idea if the reasons for it are presented first. As you read the following paragraph, think about the overall impact of the supporting ideas. Their purpose is to convince the reader that the main idea in the last sentence should be accepted.

> Last week there was a head-on collision at Huntington and Canton streets. Just a month ago a pedestrian was struck there. Fortunately, she was only slightly injured. In the past year there have been more accidents there than at any other corner in the city. In fact, nearly 10 percent of all city accidents occur there. This intersection is dangerous, and a traffic signal should be installed there before a life is lost.

The details in the paragraph progress from least important to most important. They achieve their full effect in the main idea statement at the end.

In many cases, the main idea is not expressed in a single sentence. In these cases, the reader is called upon to interpret all of the ideas expressed and decide upon a main idea. Read the following paragraph:

> The American author Jack London was once a pupil at the Cole Grammar School in Oakland, California. Each morning the class sang a song. When the teacher noticed that Jack wouldn't sing, she sent him to the principal. He returned to class with a note. It said that he could be excused from singing if he would write an essay every morning.

In this paragraph the reader has to interpret the individual ideas and decide on a main idea. This main idea seems reasonable: Jack London's career as a writer began with a "punishment" in grammar school.

Understanding the concept of the main idea and knowing how to find it is important. Transferring that understanding to your reading and study is also important.

Beetlemania

Of all known species of animals in the world, about 20 percent are beetles. There are more species of beetles than of any other kind of insect; the beetle family constitutes the largest group of insects. It includes almost one third of a million recognized species.

Beetles are found throughout all continents except Antarctica. That region is too cold for their survival. Most species are land insects, although species such as the water beetle have become adapted to water environments. Beetle species vary in size. Some may be only about 0.01 inch (0.025 centimeter) long, whereas species such as the tropical rhinoceros beetles and goliath beetles may reach lengths of 4 to 6 inches (10 to 15 centimeters).

Beetles display a remarkable array of colors, forms, and habits. They may be plain black or have brownish patterns that serve as camouflage against certain types of wood or soil. Some beetles are brilliant orange, red, or yellow. Others are iridescent green or blue, or have a metallic sheen. The antennae of certain beetles are large and ornate. Some stag beetles have enlarged, hooked mandibles, or lower jaws, that are almost as long as the beetle itself. Male rhinoceros beetles have huge horns projecting over their heads. The shapes of beetles' bodies also vary—from round to elongate, and from flattened to domed or cylindrical.

Beetles can be very destructive to plants and farm crops. Members of the family of beetles known as weevils, or snout beetles, are notorious agricultural pests. They have specialized, elongated heads and down-curved snouts with mouthparts at the end. These special features aid them in their attack on plants. Plant materials and products such as wood, paper, and fabrics are food for some beetles. The larvae of certain beetles can also be highly destructive, feeding on clothing and carpets. They have even been known to devour plant and animal specimens on display in museums.

Other species of beetles are of great value to humans. Some species prey on other destructive insect pests. Ladybugs, for example, destroy untold numbers of aphids each year, thus protecting a wide variety of flowers and vegetables. Many other beetles play more subtle but equally important roles. Dung beetles, or tumblebugs, eat vast quantities of dung in livestock areas. Carrion beetles are scavengers whose larvae feed on dead animals. And like other insects such as butterflies and bees, many beetles pollinate flowers.

Reading Time _____

Recalling Facts

1. Of all known species of animals in the world, about
   - ❑ a. 10 percent are beetles.
   - ❑ b. 20 percent are beetles.
   - ❑ c. 30 percent are beetles.

2. Beetles are found throughout all continents except
   - ❑ a. Africa.
   - ❑ b. Antarctica.
   - ❑ c. America.

3. Most species of beetles are
   - ❑ a. black.
   - ❑ b. land insects.
   - ❑ c. destructive.

4. Ladybugs are considered valuable beetles because
   - ❑ a. they prey on aphids.
   - ❑ b. of their bright color.
   - ❑ c. they eat plants.

5. The rhinoceros beetle is noted for its
   - ❑ a. color.
   - ❑ b. tail.
   - ❑ c. horns.

Understanding Ideas

6. The article wants you to understand that
   - ❑ a. there is no "typical" beetle.
   - ❑ b. most beetles look alike.
   - ❑ c. beetles are mostly less than 1 inch in length.

7. You can conclude from the article that beetles are
   - ❑ a. mostly pests.
   - ❑ b. mostly valuable.
   - ❑ c. both valuable and destructive.

8. Beetles have developed different characteristics, which suggests that
   - ❑ a. beetles are highly adaptable insects.
   - ❑ b. they can be found anywhere.
   - ❑ c. they are very intelligent.

9. Whether beetles are considered helpful or harmful is largely dependent on
   - ❑ a. what they look like.
   - ❑ b. what they feed on.
   - ❑ c. whether they are helpful to other insects.

10. You can conclude from the article that beetles feed mainly on
    - ❑ a. animals.
    - ❑ b. plants and other insects.
    - ❑ c. other beetles.

In the 1960s an immigrant to Australia named George Bornemissza looked out at a field where cattle had been grazing. It was full of cow dung—so full, in fact, that the dung had smothered the grass. Bornemissza remembered the cow pastures of his native Hungary—neat, tidy, and full of rich grass. The difference, he soon realized, was that in Australia, where cows were introduced relatively late in its history, there were no dung beetles.

Dung beetles, members of the scarab family, perform an important service to humankind. They carry away dung and bury it. They lay their eggs in the buried balls of dung, and the larvae feed on the dung until they emerge as adult beetles. The buried dung balls then decompose into manure, enriching the soil by releasing nitrogen and other nutrients important for plant growth. Furthermore, by burying the dung, the beetles also help reduce the numbers of disease-ridden flies that usually reproduce in it.

Bornemissza set out to convince the Australian government to import dung beetles from Europe and Africa to deal with the cow dung in Australia. In 1970 he won government approval and began importing dung beetle eggs. Today, thanks to Bornemissza's persistence, 32 different kinds of dung beetles are at home in Australia, helping to restore its grasslands and reduce the fly population.

1. **Recognizing Words in Context**

   Find the word *decompose* in the passage. One definition below is a *synonym* for that word; it means the same or almost the same thing. One definition is an *antonym*; it has the opposite or nearly opposite meaning. The other has a completely different meaning. Label the definitions S for *synonym*, A for *antonym*, and D for *different*.

   _____ a. reappear
   _____ b. disintegrate
   _____ c. solidify

2. **Distinguishing Fact from Opinion**

   Two of the statements below present *facts*, which can be proved correct. The other statement is an *opinion*, which expresses someone's thoughts or beliefs. Label the statements F for *fact* and O for *opinion*.

   _____ a. Imported dung beetles now live in Australia.
   _____ b. Dung beetles perform an important service to humankind.
   _____ c. Dung beetles lay their eggs in balls of dung.

3. Keeping Events in Order

Label the statements below 1, 2, and 3 to show the order in which the events happened.

_____ a. Dung beetles established themselves in Australia.

_____ b. The Australian government approved the importation of dung beetle eggs.

_____ c. George Bornemissza moved from Hungary to Australia.

4. Making Correct Inferences

Two of the statements below are correct *inferences,* or reasonable guesses. They are based on information in the passage. The other statement is an incorrect, or faulty, inference. Label the statements C for *correct* inference and F for *faulty* inference.

_____ a. Bornemissza was wrong in believing that Australia needed dung beetles.

_____ b. In Australia, the lack of dung beetles caused problems in the pastures.

_____ c. Bornemissza's project was successful.

5. Understanding Main Ideas

One of the statements below expresses the main idea of the passage. One statement is too general, or too broad. The other explains only part of the passage; it is too narrow. Label the statements M for *main idea,* B for *too broad,* and N for *too narrow.*

_____ a. Australian pastures were full of cow dung because there were no dung beetles to deal with it.

_____ b. George Bornemissza solved Australia's cow dung problem by introducing dung beetles.

_____ c. Dung beetles are useful insects.

Correct Answers, Part A _____

Correct Answers, Part B _____

Total Correct Answers _____

A Daily Record

A diary is a daily personal record. In it the writer is free to record anything at all. This may include events, comments, ideas, reading notes, or any subject on one's mind. Diaries may be kept for various purposes—to record the experienes of one's life so as not to forget them, to record ideas that might prove useful, or simply to express oneself through the medium of the printed word.

In past centuries people in public life often kept diaries. These have become valuable sources of fact and interpretation for later historians. The private, candid observations set down in these personal journals often provide truer pictures of an age than do official records or other books, which may have been censored during that time. For the most part, these diaries were never intended to be read by others. The entries were made simply as aids to memory or as a form of relaxation.

In modern times, however, politicians and other important people realize that their diaries will likely be read by historians or, in published form, by the public. Thus they may make entries with these readers in mind. As a result, their diaries may lose the confidential, intimate nature of older ones. On the other hand, their entries may tend to be more complete and self-explanatory.

The most famous diary ever written in English was that kept by Samuel Pepys. A civilian official of the British navy, Pepys made regular entries between 1660 and 1669. His diary starts at the beginning of the Restoration period in English history and describes many of the court intrigues and scandals of his day. The diary reveals Pepys as a man with many human weaknesses but one who was honest with himself. He wrote his entries in a combined code and shorthand that was not solved until more than 100 years after his death.

The most famous diary of the 20th century was published in English in 1953 with the simple title *Diary of a Young Girl*. It is more commonly known as *The Diary of Anne Frank*. Anne was a young Jewish girl whose diary records the two years her family spent in hiding, mostly in the Netherlands, trying to escape the Nazi persecutors of the Jews. She and her family were finally caught in August 1944. She was imprisoned and died at a concentration camp in Germany in March 1945.

Reading Time _____

Recalling Facts

1. A diary is a
   - ❏ a. report on world events.
   - ❏ b. daily personal record.
   - ❏ c. documentary.

2. The most famous diary ever written in English was kept by
   - ❏ a. Samuel Johnson.
   - ❏ b. Samuel Porter.
   - ❏ c. Samuel Pepys.

3. *Diary of a Young Girl* was written
   - ❏ a. during the Civil War.
   - ❏ b. in the 19th century.
   - ❏ c. in the 1940s.

4. Anne Frank's diary describes
   - ❏ a. the years her family spent hiding from the Nazis.
   - ❏ b. a German concentration camp.
   - ❏ c. the life of an average young girl.

5. Samuel Pepys was a
   - ❏ a. shoemaker.
   - ❏ b. civilian officer of the British navy.
   - ❏ c. member of the British court.

Understanding Ideas

6. Diaries of the past may give a truer picture of an age than published books because
   - ❏ a. diaries are uncensored.
   - ❏ b. published books gave only one point of view.
   - ❏ c. amateur writers were more thorough than professional writers.

7. Today's diarists may not be as confidential as those of the past because
   - ❏ a. they expect that their diaries will be read by others.
   - ❏ b. they have more secrets to hide.
   - ❏ c. people today are harsher critics.

8. You can conclude from the article that Samuel Pepys wrote his diary in code and shorthand because he
   - ❏ a. was fond of mysteries.
   - ❏ b. did not want his diary to be read by the wrong people.
   - ❏ c. could not write proper English.

9. It is likely that most people keep diaries in order to
   - ❏ a. become famous.
   - ❏ b. keep personal records.
   - ❏ c. practice their writing skills.

10. You can conclude from the article that Anne Frank
    - ❏ a. did not expect her diary to be published.
    - ❏ b. wrote her diary for publication after her death.
    - ❏ c. gave an accurate picture of life in the Netherlands.

Monday, September 17, 1492—After dawn we saw much weed, very delicate. It appeared to be river weed, and it came from the west. I found a live crab in the weed, which I took to be a sure sign of land.

Wednesday, October 10—The men are complaining about the long voyage and wish to turn back. I cheered them as best I could. At length I told them it was useless to complain. I intend to go to the Indies, and I shall continue until I find them.

Friday, October 12—At two hours after midnight, land appeared. We lay-to waiting for daylight. Presently we saw naked people gathering on the shore. I went ashore in my barge and broke out the royal standard. I called to my captains and to Rodrigo de Escobedo, secretary of the fleet, to witness as I formally took possession of this land for the King and Queen.

I gave to the people glass beads, which they hung on their necks, and many other things of slight value, in which they took much pleasure. They remained so much our friends that it was a marvel. They ought to be good servants and of good skill. I will carry off six of them at my departure to bring to their Highnesses.

1. **Recognizing Words in Context**

   Find the word *slight* in the passage. One definition below is a *synonym* for that word; it means the same or almost the same thing. One definition is an *antonym;* it has the opposite or nearly opposite meaning. The other has a completely different meaning. Label the definitions S for *synonym,* A for *antonym,* and D for *different.*

   _____ a. little
   _____ b. slim
   _____ c. great

2. **Distinguishing Fact from Opinion**

   Two of the statements below present *facts,* which can be proved correct. The other statement is an *opinion,* which expresses someone's thoughts or beliefs. Label the statements F for *fact* and O for *opinion.*

   _____ a. Columbus was a cruel, heartless man.
   _____ b. Columbus gave the people glass beads.
   _____ c. The native people were friendly toward Columbus and his men.

3. Keeping Events in Order

Label the statements below 1, 2, and 3 to show the order in which the events happened.

_____ a. Land appeared two hours after midnight.

_____ b. The crew complained about the length of the voyage.

_____ c. Columbus and his crew began to see signs of land, such as weeds with a live crab in it.

4. Making Correct Inferences

Two of the statements below are correct *inferences*, or reasonable guesses. They are based on information in the passage. The other statement is an incorrect, or faulty, inference. Label the statements C for *correct* inference and F for *faulty* inference.

_____ a. Columbus had landed in the Indies.

_____ b. Columbus's crew might have rebelled if they had not found land.

_____ c. Columbus did not respect the rights of the native people.

5. Understanding Main Ideas

One of the statements below expresses the main idea of the passage. One statement is too general, or too broad. The other explains only part of the passage; it is too narrow. Label the statements M for *main idea*, B for *too broad*, and N for *too narrow*.

_____ a. After a long voyage and resistance from his crew, Columbus reached land.

_____ b. Columbus claimed the land in the name of the King and Queen.

_____ c. Christopher Columbus was a determined explorer.

Correct Answers, Part A _____

Correct Answers, Part B _____

Total Correct Answers _____

The skill of fencing, or fighting with a sword, has been practiced in all parts of the world for many centuries. Men, and sometimes women, fought battles with many different types of swords. After duels were forbidden by law, sport fencing remained popular. Three different kinds of fencing are practiced today, each named for the type of sword used: foil, epee, and saber. The objective of fencing is to touch the valid target with the point of the foil or epee, or with the cutting edge and point of the saber.

The three swords that are used in fencing have evolved from different weapons of combat. The foil developed from the light French court sword and was also the practice weapon of the 17th century. The epee evolved from the 16th-century rapier used by the French musketeers. The saber is a light, slender, flexible weapon that derives from the slashing cavalry sword of the 18th-century Hungarian hussars.

Today men and women fence with all three weapons and compete individually and in teams. Each weapon requires slight variations of style, technique, and rules. Each of the three weapons has a different scoring target. The foil scores anywhere on the torso. The epee targets the total body. The saber targets the body from the hips up, including the arms and the mask.

When fencing with electrical equipment, the foil fencer must wear an outer vest made of metallic cloth and an electrical body cord. The epee fencer uses just the electrical body cord. Both weapons are wired. When the point of the foil depresses on the outer vest, the electrical circuit is activated, the scoring apparatus buzzes, and a colored light goes on. When it depresses on the other parts of the body (off target), a white light goes on. When the point of the epee is depressed on the target, a colored light is turned on. The electrical apparatus acts as the jury for the director, or referee.

All equipment and protective clothing are standardized. Dress includes a fencing jacket, wire-mesh mask with proper bib, leather glove, trousers or breeches and stockings, underarm protector, breastplates for women, and protective athletic supporter for men. These items must be worn at all times when fencing at any level of competition. White is usually the color of fencing uniforms and equipment. In recent years, however, the use of light pastel colors has become acceptable.

Reading Time _____

Recalling Facts

1. The different kinds of fencing practiced today are named for
   - ❏ a. famous fencers.
   - ❏ b. the type of swords used.
   - ❏ c. the type of clothing worn.

2. A fencer wanting to target the entire body would use
   - ❏ a. an epee.
   - ❏ b. a foil.
   - ❏ c. a saber.

3. Fencing equipment and clothing are
   - ❏ a. always white.
   - ❏ b. standardized.
   - ❏ c. up to the individual.

4. When foil fencing with electrical equipment, different colored lights turn on to indicate
   - ❏ a. where on the body a sword has scored.
   - ❏ b. what kind of sword is used.
   - ❏ c. when the referee must vote.

5. All competitive fencers must wear
   - ❏ a. full armor.
   - ❏ b. breastplates.
   - ❏ c. wire-mesh masks.

Understanding Ideas

6. You can conclude from the article that when an electrical apparatus is used in fencing, it aids in determining
   - ❏ a. the length of a match.
   - ❏ b. the winning fencer.
   - ❏ c. who is cheating.

7. It is likely that special clothing is required in competition to
   - ❏ a. prevent wounding.
   - ❏ b. inhibit fencers.
   - ❏ c. protect against electrical charges.

8. From the article you can conclude that duels were outlawed because
   - ❏ a. people were being killed.
   - ❏ b. swords were too expensive.
   - ❏ c. they were used to settle arguments.

9. It is likely that scoring targets differ for each type of sword because
   - ❏ a. it makes fencing competitions more interesting.
   - ❏ b. the swords themselves have different characteristics.
   - ❏ c. the size of the competitors changes.

10. The article wants you to understand that fencing
    - ❏ a. has changed from a type of fighting to a competitive sport.
    - ❏ b. has lost its popularity.
    - ❏ c. is making a comeback.

Only 20 years old, Cliff Bayer is America's best fencer. He is also one of the best fencers in the world. Bayer began fencing as a small child. By the time he was in his early teens, he was flying alone to fencing matches in Europe.

At 17, while still in high school, he became the youngest United States National Fencing Champion. He took a year off from school to prepare for the 1996 Olympic Games, and was ranked number one foil fencer on the United States Olympic Fencing Team.

Olympic competition, Bayer learned, is different from other competitions. The day of the Olympic match was hot, and the competition took place before a huge, boisterous audience. Bayer was nervous and distracted. He lost in the first round, only three minutes into the competition.

He was upset but not discouraged. He knew that his best years as a fencer were still ahead of him. He returned home and started college while continuing to fence competitively.

In 1996 Bayer won a Bronze Medal in the World Under-Twenty Championship in Spain. Today he attends college, works, practices, and competes with his goal firmly in place—a medal at the Olympics in the year 2000.

1. **Recognizing Words in Context**

   Find the word *boisterous* in the passage. One definition below is a *synonym* for that word; it means the same or almost the same thing. One definition is an *antonym;* it has the opposite or nearly opposite meaning. The other has a completely different meaning. Label the definitions S for *synonym,* A for *antonym,* and D for *different.*

   _____ a. clamorous
   _____ b. subdued
   _____ c. disinterested

2. **Distinguishing Fact from Opinion**

   Two of the statements below present *facts,* which can be proved correct. The other statement is an *opinion,* which expresses someone's thoughts or beliefs. Label the statements F for *fact* and O for *opinion.*

   _____ a. Bayer was United States National Fencing Champion at 17.
   _____ b. Cliff Bayer is America's best fencer.
   _____ c. Bayer won a Bronze Medal in a world championship competition.

3. Keeping Events in Order

Label the statements below 1, 2, and 3 to show the order in which the events happened.

_____ a. Bayer started college.

_____ b. Bayer competed in the Olympics.

_____ c. At 17, Bayer became United States National Fencing Champion.

4. Making Correct Inferences

Two of the statements below are correct *inferences,* or reasonable guesses. They are based on information in the passage. The other statement is an incorrect, or faulty, inference. Label the statements C for *correct* inference and F for *faulty* inference.

_____ a. Fencing is the only thing in Bayer's life.

_____ b. Bayer is confident of his skills.

_____ c. Bayer works hard at his sport.

5. Understanding Main Ideas

One of the statements below expresses the main idea of the passage. One statement is too general, or too broad. The other explains only part of the passage; it is too narrow. Label the statements M for *main idea,* B for *too broad,* and N for *too narrow.*

_____ a. Cliff Bayer is America's youngest fencing champion.

_____ b. Cliff Bayer has an impressive record as a fencer, despite his young age.

_____ c. America's Olympic sports include fencing.

Correct Answers, Part A _____

Correct Answers, Part B _____

Total Correct Answers _____

Guy de Maupassant

A French master of the short story, Guy de Maupassant had a special gift for dramatic swiftness and naturalness, exemplified in his most famous story, "The Necklace."

Henri-Rene-Albert-Guy de Maupassant was born on August 5, 1850, near Dieppe in the French province of Normandy. His parents separated when he was 11 and he remained with his mother and younger brother at Etretat on the English Channel. In his youth he was fond of fishing and boating and of writing verse.

Maupassant was educated at the Rouen lycee and at the University of Caen. After serving in the Franco-Prussian War, he went to Paris where his father found him a job as a government clerk. He spent much of his spare time writing. In Paris Maupassant attended literary gatherings at the house of the novelist Gustave Flaubert, an old friend of his mother. For 10 years Flaubert tutored the young man, teaching him patience and the need for acute observation and realistic description. Maupassant was also influenced by Émile Zola, leader of the new naturalistic school of fiction writing.

Maupassant wrote about people and events he had known. At 30 he was so successful as a short-story writer that he gave up his government job. His earliest stories deal with the people of Normandy and scenes he knew so well in his youth—peasants, townspeople, and life by the banks of the River Seine. Later he wrote a few war stories and a group of tales about Paris. His travels on the French and Italian Rivieras, in other parts of Italy, and in North Africa furnished backgrounds for more stories.

Some of Maupassant's stories have surprise endings; others conclude as the reader expects they will. As a realist, Maupassant's stories have little sentimentality, but do not lack sympathy for his characters. His general attitude was cynical and he was often melancholy. His friends nicknamed him "the gloomy bull."

Maupassant's last years were tragic. He became increasingly erratic, and early in 1892 he tried to commit suicide. His mother reluctantly had him placed in a mental institution in Paris, where he died on July 6, 1893.

Maupassant's enormous output of short stories—nearly 300—appeared in various collections. Although noted for his short stories, Maupassant produced novels as well. His novels include *Une Vie* and *Pierre et Jean*. The hero of his novel *Bel-Ami,* published in 1885, is an ambitious rascal.

Reading Time _____

Recalling Facts

1. Maupassant is known as a master of
   - ❏ a. the short story.
   - ❏ b. poetry.
   - ❏ c. the novel.

2. Maupassant's most famous story is titled
   - ❏ a. "The Parasol."
   - ❏ b. "The Necklace."
   - ❏ c. "Une Vie."

3. The two greatest influences on Maupassant's writing were
   - ❏ a. Paris and the River Seine.
   - ❏ b. The French and Italian Rivieras.
   - ❏ c. Flaubert and Zola.

4. To pursue a writing career, Maupassant gave up
   - ❏ a. a government job.
   - ❏ b. fishing and boating.
   - ❏ c. traveling.

5. Maupassant died
   - ❏ a. a wealthy and happy man.
   - ❏ b. of malaria.
   - ❏ c. in a mental institution.

Understanding Ideas

6. From the article you can conclude that Maupassant
   - ❏ a. discovered he enjoyed writing while living in Paris.
   - ❏ b. had always enjoyed writing.
   - ❏ c. never considered writing as a career until he met Flaubert and Zola.

7. Maupassant frequently wrote about the people and places of his youth, suggesting that he
   - ❏ a. had an unhappy childhood.
   - ❏ b. felt comfortable writing about things he knew well.
   - ❏ c. was afraid to travel.

8. Maupassant's stories have little sentimentality, which suggests that he
   - ❏ a. was a warm, friendly person.
   - ❏ b. focused on the harsh realities of life.
   - ❏ c. disliked writing about people.

9. From the article you can conclude that Maupassant preferred writing
   - ❏ a. fiction.
   - ❏ b. nonfiction.
   - ❏ c. verse.

10. You can conclude from the article that, given the success of Maupassant's writing, readers of short stories enjoy
   - ❏ a. naturalness and realistic description.
   - ❏ b. a surprise ending.
   - ❏ c. great detail.

4 B   Émile Zola and the Dreyfus Affair

The French novelist Émile Zola (1840–1902), leader of the naturalist school of writing, produced frank novels that stressed the effect of heredity and the environment on people's actions. Naturalists believed that writers should portray the brutality of industrial life. Zola's outspoken novel *Germinal* described the degradation endured by miners working and living in the inhuman conditions of northern French mines. Zola's work influenced such other writers as Guy de Maupassant.

Zola expressed his beliefs and ideals in his life, not just in novels. His involvement in what became known as the Dreyfus Affair caused him to flee France for brief exile in England. The affair began in 1894 with the court martial for treason of Alfred Dreyfus, a French army officer and a Jew. Convicted on scanty evidence of spying for Germany, Dreyfus was sentenced to Devil's Island for life. His case resulted in a wave of anti-Semitism in France. In support of reopening the case, Zola wrote a famous pamphlet, *J'Accuse,* in 1898. Eventually an officer who had forged the evidence that convicted Dreyfus confessed and committed suicide. Dreyfus was given clemency in 1899 and fully cleared in 1906, thanks to the efforts of Zola and other supporters.

1. **Recognizing Words in Context**

   Find the word *scanty* in the passage. One definition below is a *synonym* for that word; it means the same or almost the same thing. One definition is an *antonym;* it has the opposite or nearly opposite meaning. The other has a completely different meaning. Label the definitions S for *synonym,* A for *antonym,* and D for *different.*

   _____ a. frugal
   _____ b. slight
   _____ c. considerable

2. **Distinguishing Fact from Opinion**

   Two of the statements below present *facts,* which can be proved correct. The other statement is an *opinion,* which expresses someone's thoughts or beliefs. Label the statements F for *fact* and O for *opinion.*

   _____ a. Émile Zola was a leader of the naturalist school of writing in France.
   _____ b. Zola's work influenced that of other writers, such as Guy de Maupassant.
   _____ c. Zola should have kept to his fiction and stayed out of the Dreyfus Affair.

3. **Keeping Events in Order**

   Label the statements below 1, 2, and 3 to show the order in which the events happened.

   _____ a. Alfred Dreyfus was tried for treason and convicted.

   _____ b. Dreyfus was given clemency and eventually cleared.

   _____ c. Émile Zola wrote a letter in support of Dreyfus.

4. **Making Correct Inferences**

   Two of the statements below are correct *inferences*, or reasonable guesses. They are based on information in the passage. The other statement is an incorrect, or faulty, inference. Label the statements C for *correct* inference and F for *faulty* inference.

   _____ a. Zola's pamphlet, *J'Accuse*, helped get the Dreyfus case reopened.

   _____ b. France is an anti-Semitic nation.

   _____ c. Zola believed that Dreyfus was innocent.

5. **Understanding Main Ideas**

   One of the statements below expresses the main idea of the passage. One statement is too general, or too broad. The other explains only part of the passage; it is too narrow. Label the statements M for *main idea,* B for *too broad,* and N for *too narrow.*

   _____ a. French novelist Émile Zola helped obtain the freedom of unjustly convicted army officer Alfred Dreyfus.

   _____ b. Anti-Semitism following the Dreyfus Affair opened political and social divisions that troubled France.

   _____ c. Émile Zola wrote a pamphlet, *J'Accuse,* in support of Alfred Dreyfus.

Correct Answers, Part A _____

Correct Answers, Part B _____

Total Correct Answers _____

Building Roads

Before the invention of the automobile, primitive trails and roads generally followed paths made at random by animals and people as they walked about. Today, engineers try to locate the best possible site for a road. They design the road well in advance in order to take into consideration as many environmental and traffic factors as possible. They then present their results in a construction plan, leaving nothing to chance.

The first step in building a road is to select and obtain the right-of-way. This is the strip of land that will become the road with all its signs, light poles, barriers, and interchanges. The right-of-way can be the most expensive item when building roads and motorways through cities. Homes and businesses may have to be bought and demolished.

Planners carefully test the soil under a proposed roadway to make sure it has the strength to carry the pavement and traffic. With modern testing equipment, engineers can carry out tests right at the site and obtain the results within a few minutes.

Airplanes and satellites are used to survey the right-of-way. Their cameras and instruments can determine the type of rock or soil in any location. Photographs reveal sources of road-building materials and provide an overall view of the region. Aerial photography provides detailed maps that planners use to select the final route of the highway. Tests determine what kinds of gravel, rock, and sands are available for building the roadway. Other tests are used to detect any weaknesses that might complicate construction or shorten the life of the road.

Until the late 1900s road planners and builders would sometimes build new roads without regard for the effects of noise, air, and water pollution. They failed to see how soil erosion might harm the local population and wildlife. Now there is a law that requires all agencies to study the possible consequences of road construction. They are required to list the consequences in an environmental impact statement. Groups who object to the proposed road can voice their objections at public hearings. Citizens can stall construction until their objections and questions are answered. Getting approval for construction of new highways in urban areas is especially difficult. It usually means demolishing existing homes and businesses to make room for the roadway. Many freeways and highways that were planned to run through major cities in the 1950s and 1960s were canceled because of opposition.

Reading Time _____

Recalling Facts

1. The first step in building a road is to
   - ❏ a. test the soil under the roadway.
   - ❏ b. hire a construction crew.
   - ❏ c. select and obtain the right-of-way.

2. Maps of potential road sites are provided by
   - ❏ a. aerial photographers.
   - ❏ b. environmentalists.
   - ❏ c. local homeowners.

3. Soil under a potential roadway is tested for its
   - ❏ a. richness.
   - ❏ b. dryness.
   - ❏ c. strength.

4. The purpose of public hearings prior to road construction is to
   - ❏ a. hear objections about the construction.
   - ❏ b. present construction plans.
   - ❏ c. put the public on trial.

5. An environmental impact statement
   - ❏ a. lists the possible consequences of construction on the environment.
   - ❏ b. provides approval of construction of new highways.
   - ❏ c. discusses the impact of the environment on construction.

Understanding Ideas

6. Environmental factors are
   - ❏ a. important considerations in building a road.
   - ❏ b. considered after a road is built.
   - ❏ c. disregarded when building a road.

7. You can conclude from the article that opposition to a road
   - ❏ a. is usually ignored.
   - ❏ b. is taken very seriously.
   - ❏ c. at most can stall construction.

8. You can conclude from the article that the cost of a right-of-way is dependent on
   - ❏ a. the size of a city.
   - ❏ b. the number of homes and buildings that need to be demolished.
   - ❏ c. how many citizens object.

9. You can conclude from the article that the main force behind modern road construction was the
   - ❏ a. railroad.
   - ❏ b. invention of the automobile.
   - ❏ c. evolution of cities.

10. The article wants you to understand that road construction today is
    - ❏ a. strictly an economic undertaking.
    - ❏ b. considered from every possible angle.
    - ❏ c. left up to scientists.

Working on the Road

Maria Gonzales is a flagperson on a road crew repairing a state highway. She reports to work before 7:00 A.M. to ride with the crew to the work area. Maria goes immediately to her place; she must control traffic while the area is being set up. It is still chilly, but later it will be blistering hot. At least it's not raining. Her crew works in all conditions.

Today they close one lane of a two-lane highway around a curve. Maria isn't able to see her partner at the other end. She stays in contact by radio. Since traffic in both directions uses one lane, she must make sure the road is clear before starting oncoming traffic. She must be vigilant and make no mistakes.

Breaks are short. Standing all day is hard, but even when there is no traffic, she cannot sit down or relax. The job is too important.

At end of day, Maria is the last to leave. The road must be clear and the road cones stowed before both lanes are opened. She's tired, but she considers herself lucky, because it's a good job and she's well paid.

1. Recognizing Words in Context

Find the word *vigilant* in the passage. One definition below is a *synonym* for that word; it means the same or almost the same thing. One definition is an *antonym;* it has the opposite or nearly opposite meaning. The other has a completely different meaning. Label the definitions S for *synonym*, A for *antonym,* and D for *different.*

_____ a. casual
_____ b. watchful
_____ c. practical

2. Distinguishing Fact from Opinion

Two of the statements below present *facts,* which can be proved correct. The other statement is an *opinion,* which expresses someone's thoughts or beliefs. Label the statements F for *fact* and O for *opinion.*

_____ a. Maria's day starts before 7:00 A.M.
_____ b. The road crew works in all weather conditions.
_____ c. Road work is a good job.

3. Keeping Events in Order

Label the statements below 1, 2, and 3 to show the order in which the events happened.

_____ a. The road crew closes one lane of a two-lane highway.

_____ b. Maria waits to leave the job until both lanes are opened.

_____ c. Maria rides to the work area.

4. Making Correct Inferences

Two of the statements below are correct *inferences,* or reasonable guesses. They are based on information in the passage. The other statement is an incorrect, or faulty, inference. Label the statements C for *correct* inference and F for *faulty* inference.

_____ a. The work of a flagperson is physically demanding.

_____ b. Road work is easy.

_____ c. A flagperson must be alert at all times.

5. Understanding Main Ideas

One of the statements below expresses the main idea of the passage. One statement is too general, or too broad. The other explains only part of the passage; it is too narrow. Label the statements M for *main idea,* B for *too broad,* and N for *too narrow.*

_____ a. Women now work on road crews.

_____ b. Unable to see her partner around a curve, Maria must stay in touch by radio.

_____ c. Working as a flagperson, Maria Gonzales puts in a full and demanding day.

Correct Answers, Part A _____

Correct Answers, Part B _____

Total Correct Answers _____

Though they may look fairly solid, clouds are only collections of water droplets, ice crystals, or mixtures of both. Clouds are formed by natural processes acting on moisture in the air. This moisture is constantly renewed by evaporation. Evaporation is the escape of water molecules into the air as vapor. Water evaporates from land surfaces and from the bodies of water that cover about 71 percent of the Earth's surface. Precipitation in the form of rain or snow in turn renews the surface water lost to evaporation, completing a cycle. The amount of water vapor that air can hold depends on the air's temperature. The cooler the air, the smaller the amount of water it can hold.

When air is cooled enough, some of the water vapor will condense to form a visible mass of tiny droplets. The condensation of droplets from water vapor depends on the presence in the atmosphere of minute particles. Common sources of such particles are dust, grains of salt from ocean spray, and particles from fires and volcanic eruptions.

If condensation from water vapor to droplets occurs on the ground it is called dew, which may be observed early in the morning on grass or flowers. If it happens near the ground it is called fog or mist. When it occurs in the sky it is called clouds.

When air rises it becomes cooler; therefore, when moist air is forced to rise, as for example wind blowing up a mountainside, clouds are likely to form. Thus the windward sides of mountainous lands are often more cloudy and receive more precipitation than the opposite sides. Air is also forced upward by intense heating of land. That is why areas at or near the equator are nearly always cloudy during the hottest part of the day.

Since early times people have observed the ceaseless formation and disappearance of clouds. By observing cloud shapes and patterns of movement, it is possible to forecast changes in weather.

Clouds can be grouped into three basic categories. Cirrus clouds, wispy clouds that form high in the sky from ice crystals, nearly always indicate an end to clear weather. Cumulus clouds are puffy white clouds with a flat base formed by rising bubbles of warm air. They are common on hot summer days. Stratus clouds form in layers that can reach across a whole sky and often bring drizzling rain or light snow.

Reading Time _____

Recalling Facts

1. Clouds are collections of water droplets, ice crystals, or
   - ❏ a. minute particles.
   - ❏ b. smoke.
   - ❏ c. a mixture of both.

2. The escape of water molecules into the air as vapor is called
   - ❏ a. precipitation.
   - ❏ b. evaporation.
   - ❏ c. condensation.

3. Condensation from water vapor to droplets on the ground is called
   - ❏ a. dew.
   - ❏ b. clouds.
   - ❏ c. fog.

4. Clouds are likely to form when
   - ❏ a. cool air sinks to the ground.
   - ❏ b. moist air is forced to rise.
   - ❏ c. ocean spray forms in the atmosphere.

5. The amount of water vapor that air can hold depends on the air's
   - ❏ a. density.
   - ❏ b. movement.
   - ❏ c. temperature.

Understanding Ideas

6. Warm air can hold
   - ❏ a. no water.
   - ❏ b. less water than cool air.
   - ❏ c. more water than cool air.

7. You can conclude from the article that dew usually forms during the night because
   - ❏ a. water evaporates more at night.
   - ❏ b. moist air close to the ground cools at night.
   - ❏ c. a light, drizzling rain often falls during the night.

8. People are probably fascinated by clouds because they
   - ❏ a. constantly change shape.
   - ❏ b. contain water.
   - ❏ c. are part of the water cycle.

9. You can conclude from the article that the three basic types of cloud formations
   - ❏ a. can be further broken down into combinations of these three.
   - ❏ b. are the only types that can form in Earth's atmosphere.
   - ❏ c. are the only visible formations among others that cannot be observed.

10. The crew of a sailboat far from shore would feel most secure if the sky held
    - ❏ a. cirrus clouds.
    - ❏ b. cumulus clouds.
    - ❏ c. stratus clouds.

Forming a Cloud

The water in earth's lakes, rivers, and oceans is always evaporating, turning into water vapor, tiny particles of water that we cannot see. As water evaporates, it is taken up by the air next to it. How much water the air can hold depends on the temperature of the air. Warm air can hold more water than cold air, which is why humidity can be so bothersome in summer.

As the sun warms the ground, it also warms the air near the ground. This warm air rises, carrying with it the tiny droplets of moisture that have evaporated from the earth's surface. When the air rises, however, it cools, and can now hold less moisture. The moisture in the cooler air condenses, turning back into water droplets. Those water droplets are the clouds we see.

As the clouds rise and thicken and the air around them gets colder, some of the droplets become ice crystals. Now too heavy to be supported by the air, they tumble out of the cloud, returning to the earth as rain or snow and replenishing the rivers, lakes, and seas from which they originally came.

1. **Recognizing Words in Context**

   Find the word *replenishing* in the passage. One definition below is a *synonym* for that word; it means the same or almost the same thing. One definition is an *antonym*; it has the opposite or nearly opposite meaning. The other has a completely different meaning. Label the definitions S for *synonym*, A for *antonym*, and D for *different*.

   _____ a. emptying
   _____ b. refilling
   _____ c. answering

2. **Distinguishing Fact from Opinion**

   Two of the statements below present *facts*, which can be proved correct. The other statement is an *opinion*, which expresses someone's thoughts or beliefs. Label the statements F for *fact* and O for *opinion*.

   _____ a. Warm air holds more moisture than cool air.
   _____ b. As air rises, it cools.
   _____ c. Humidity is bothersome in summer.

3. Keeping Events in Order

Label the statements below 1, 2, and 3 to show the order in which the events happened.

_____ a. Warm air at the earth's surface takes up moisture.

_____ b. The warm air rises, carrying the moisture with it.

_____ c. The moisture in the higher, cooler air condenses into droplets, forming clouds.

4. Making Correct Inferences

Two of the statements below are correct *inferences*, or reasonable guesses. They are based on information in the passage. The other statement is an incorrect, or faulty, inference. Label the statements C for *correct* inference and F for *faulty* inference.

_____ a. Clouds are part of a continuing natural cycle.

_____ b. We would be better off without clouds.

_____ c. Water vapor is all around us, although we cannot see it.

5. Understanding Main Ideas

One of the statements below expresses the main idea of the passage. One statement is too general, or too broad. The other explains only part of the passage; it is too narrow. Label the statements M for *main idea,* B for *too broad,* and N for *too narrow.*

_____ a. Clouds are formed from water vapor.

_____ b. How much water the air can hold depends on the temperature of the air.

_____ c. Clouds are part of a continuing cycle of evaporation, condensation, and precipitation.

Correct Answers, Part A _____

Correct Answers, Part B _____

Total Correct Answers _____

The Tale of Evangeline

In 1847 the poet Henry Wadsworth Longfellow published his popular poem "Evangeline." It tells of the wanderings of two French lovers who were separated during the historic fight for control of the North American continent. Their story focused on a region in the Atlantic provinces of Canada.

The French were the first Europeans to explore the St. Lawrence River and settle in Canada. To protect the entrance to the river they needed to hold the region around the Gulf of St. Lawrence, which they called Acadia. Acadia was made up of what is now New Brunswick, Nova Scotia, Prince Edward Island, and some parts of Newfoundland. In 1605 the French built a fort, Port Royal, in the region south of the gulf. Because of its geographical position, Acadia became involved in the struggle between the British and French for possession of North America. In 1621 James I of England granted Acadia to Sir William Alexander, who renamed it Nova Scotia. Time after time Port Royal was conquered by the English and retaken by the French. French families who settled in the area took no part in the wars. They also lived in peace with the friendly Micmac Indians of the region.

The final struggle for North America began in 1754. The English were in control of Acadia. English authorities demanded that unless the Acadians take an oath of allegiance to England, they would be deported. In 1755, about 6,000 Acadians were shipped to English colonies along the Atlantic coast, from Massachusetts to South Carolina. Some made their way to Louisiana to live with the French settlers there. Their descendants are called Cajuns, many of whom still speak a French dialect. The name *Cajun* derives from the English pronunciation of Acadian: "Acadjunn."

Evangeline, the heroine of Longfellow's poem, and her lover, Gabriel, lived in the village of Grand Pre in what is now Nova Scotia. On the day of their betrothal in 1755, the English summoned all the men of Grand Pre to the church. After being held prisoner for five days, they were herded onto ships. The next day Evangeline was exiled.

Evangeline spent the rest of her life wandering in search of her lover. Eventually she became a Sister of Mercy in Philadelphia, Pennsylvania. There, in an almshouse, she finally found Gabriel as he was dying. A statue of Evangeline stands today in a memorial park in Grand Pre.

Reading Time _____

Recalling Facts

1. Acadia included what is now
   - ❏ a. Massachusetts.
   - ❏ b. Nova Scotia.
   - ❏ c. Louisiana.

2. The struggle for the North American continent in that region involved
   - ❏ a. America and England.
   - ❏ b. Canada and America.
   - ❏ c. England and France.

3. Descendants of Acadians in Louisiana are called
   - ❏ a. French.
   - ❏ b. Creoles.
   - ❏ c. Cajuns.

4. The poem "Evangeline" was written by
   - ❏ a. Wordsworth.
   - ❏ b. Longfellow.
   - ❏ c. Poe.

5. Evangeline and her lover, Gabriel, were separated when
   - ❏ a. Acadians were deported by the English.
   - ❏ b. Acadians were deported by the French.
   - ❏ c. Acadians were deported by the Canadians.

Understanding Ideas

6. You can conclude from the article that Acadians took no part in wars because they
   - ❏ a. sided with the French.
   - ❏ b. sided with the English.
   - ❏ c. were peaceful people.

7. Acadians who refused to take an oath of allegiance to England showed
   - ❏ a. remorse.
   - ❏ b. pride in their heritage.
   - ❏ c. lack of courage.

8. If the English had lost the struggle for North America, it is likely that
   - ❏ a. Acadians would not have been deported.
   - ❏ b. the Micmac Indians would have revolted.
   - ❏ c. Americans would speak French.

9. The poem "Evangeline" commemorates
   - ❏ a. war.
   - ❏ b. tragic love.
   - ❏ c. revenge.

10. A statue of Evangeline was erected in Grand Pre, which suggests that
    - ❏ a. Evangeline was a real person.
    - ❏ b. England is much admired in Grand Pre.
    - ❏ c. the people of Grand Pre admire the spirit of the poem "Evangeline."

One spring Bouqui and Lapin agreed to farm together. Lapin suggested that they split everything equally. Bouqui would take the parts that grew under the ground, while he, Lapin, would take the parts that grew above the ground. Bouqui agreed. Lapin provided the seeds, and Bouqui did all the plowing and planting.

When the crops were ready for harvesting, Bouqui discovered that they had grown only such plants as corn, beans, cabbage, and melons. The only things underground were the roots of these plants. Lapin consoled Bouqui by telling him that he could feed the roots to his cow.

The next spring, Bouqui decided to be clever. He demanded that this year he would have all the parts that grew above the ground, and Lapin would have the parts that grew under the ground. Lapin agreed. Once again Lapin provided the seeds, and Bouqui did all the plowing and planting.

Autumn came, and Bouqui discovered that all they had grown were carrots, turnips, peanuts, and potatoes. The only things aboveground were the leaves of the plants and some inedible gourds. Lapin consoled Bouqui by telling him that he could make dippers and bowls out of all the gourds.

1. **Recognizing Words in Context**

   Find the word *grown* in the passage. One definition below is a *synonym* for that word; it means the same or almost the same thing. One definition is an *antonym;* it has the opposite or nearly opposite meaning. The other has a completely different meaning. Label the definitions S for *synonym*, A for *antonym*, and D for *different*.

   _____ a. raised
   _____ b. destroyed
   _____ c. increased

2. **Distinguishing Fact from Opinion**

   Two of the statements below present *facts,* which can be proved correct. The other statement is an *opinion,* which expresses someone's thoughts or beliefs. Label the statements F for *fact* and O for *opinion.*

   _____ a. The first year, all the vegetables grew above the ground.
   _____ b. The second year, all the vegetables grew under the ground.
   _____ c. Bouqui thought he was being clever by demanding what grew aboveground.

3. Keeping Events in Order

Label the statements below 1, 2, and 3 to show the order in which the events happened.

_____ a. Bouqui agreed to take whatever grew underground.

_____ b. Bouqui demanded whatever grew aboveground.

_____ c. All they grew were corn, beans, cabbage, and melons.

4. Making Correct Inferences

Two of the statements below are correct *inferences,* or reasonable guesses. They are based on information in the passage. The other statement is an incorrect, or faulty, inference. Label the statements C for *correct* inference and F for *faulty* inference.

_____ a. Lapin set out to cheat Bouqui of the food.

_____ b. Neither Bouqui nor Lapin knew what crops they would produce each year.

_____ c. Lapin was making fun of Bouqui, not consoling him.

5. Understanding Main Ideas

One of the statements below expresses the main idea of the passage. One statement is too general, or too broad. The other explains only part of the passage; it is too narrow. Label the statements M for *main idea,* B for *too broad,* and N for *too narrow.*

_____ a. Lapin provided the seeds, and Bouqui did the plowing and planting.

_____ b. The Cajuns have a rich folklore that reflects a variety of cultural origins.

_____ c. Lapin kept outwitting Bouqui, with whom he had agreed to farm.

Correct Answers, Part A _____

Correct Answers, Part B _____

Total Correct Answers _____

Quakers

In 1652 George Fox, standing on high Pendle Hill in England, had a vision. This was the beginning of the Religious Society of Friends, whose members are commonly called Quakers. A magistrate first used this name in Derby in 1650, when Fox was on trial for his beliefs. His followers trembled with religious excitement, and Fox bade the judge to "tremble at the word of the Lord."

George Fox believed, as the Puritans did, that the formal practices of the Church of England violated the spirit of Christianity. He taught that people could worship God directly without help from clergy, that individuals—of any race or sex—could personally receive and follow the guiding "Inner Light" within themselves. His followers refused to attend the services of the Church of England or to pay tithes for its support. They refused to take oaths on the ground that an oath recognizes a double standard of truth. They were frugal and plain in dress and speech.

The authorities persecuted the Quakers with fines, confiscation of property, and imprisonment. Nevertheless the sect flourished. In 1689 the Toleration Act ended the persecution. Meanwhile, Quakers could settle freely in America on a large grant of land given to the Quaker William Penn in 1681. A group known as the Hicksites differed in some of the beliefs and separated from the orthodox Quakers in 1827. Other divisions among Quakers also developed over the years.

Quakers still reflect the teachings of Fox. They do not sanction taking part in war because they feel that war causes spiritual damage through hatred. Most Quakers therefore refuse to serve in the military, but individuals follow their own convictions.

The Friends have no ritual, sacraments, or ordained clergy. They appoint elders and overseers to serve at their meetings. Men and women who have received a "gift" are called recorded ministers. Meetings are held in waiting silence. Members speak in prayer or testimony as the Inner Light moves them. After an hour the meeting ends with the members shaking hands.

Quakers have always been active in human rights issues. They have been instrumental in prison reform, rights for the mentally ill, the antislavery movement, rights for women, and relief service. In the 19th century Quakers in the United States founded numerous colleges and universities with an emphasis on science. Because Friends were trusted and extended credit, they also became active in banking and insurance.

Reading Time _____

Recalling Facts

1. George Fox was put on trial because
   - ❏ a. he refused to serve in the military.
   - ❏ b. he was accused of bribery.
   - ❏ c. of his religious beliefs.

2. Quakers get their name from
   - ❏ a. a judge's remark on their trembling during religious excitement.
   - ❏ b. the Church of England's order that they tremble before its authority.
   - ❏ c. the shaky handwriting of their founder, George Fox.

3. Persecution of the Quakers ended when
   - ❏ a. George Fox had a vision in 1652.
   - ❏ b. the Toleration Act was passed in 1689.
   - ❏ c. they were put on trial for their beliefs.

4. Quakers settled in America on land given to
   - ❏ a. George Fox.
   - ❏ b. William Penn.
   - ❏ c. the Religious Society of Friends.

5. After a religious meeting, Quakers
   - ❏ a. collect contributions.
   - ❏ b. have a period of silence.
   - ❏ c. shake hands.

Understanding Ideas

6. Quakers have no ordained clergy because of their belief that
   - ❏ a. clergy cause spiritual damage.
   - ❏ b. God does not exist.
   - ❏ c. people can worship God directly.

7. Why did Quakers choose to settle in America?
   - ❏ a. They could worship freely there.
   - ❏ b. They wanted to avoid fighting for England.
   - ❏ c. They wanted to establish a college there.

8. Quakers serving in the military would be
   - ❏ a. thrown out of the Religious Society of Friends.
   - ❏ b. following their own convictions.
   - ❏ c. sent to jail.

9. The article suggests that Quakers
   - ❏ a. are easily swayed in their beliefs.
   - ❏ b. have a strong moral code.
   - ❏ c. would make good scientists.

10. Several divisions among Quakers have developed over the years, which suggests that
    - ❏ a. all Quakers share the same beliefs.
    - ❏ b. Quakers differ in some of their beliefs.
    - ❏ c. Quakers are converting to other religions.

The Grimké Sisters: Quaker Reformers

Born to wealth as the daughters of a slaveholder in South Carolina, Sarah (1792–1873) and Angelina (1805–1879) Grimké recognized the evils of slavery. In order to join the antislavery cause, the Grimké sisters moved north and became Quakers.

Their personal experiences with slavery made the sisters persuasive as both speakers and writers. In 1836 Angelina published a pamphlet, *Appeal to the Christian Women of the South,* that caused a sensation throughout the country. Angelina soon became highly popular as a speaker at antislavery meetings and attracted great crowds. In 1838 she was the first woman to address a committee of the Massachusetts legislature on antislavery petitions.

From the antislavery movement to the fight for equality for women was a natural step for the Grimké sisters and other Quaker women. Angelina wrote, "Let us all first wake up the nation to lift millions of slaves of both sexes from the dust, . . . and then . . . it will be an easy matter to take millions of females from their knees and . . . transform them from babies into women." In a series of articles, Sarah Grimké wrote, "All I ask of our brethren is that they will take their feet from off our necks, and permit us to stand upright on the ground which God has designed us to occupy."

1. Recognizing Words in Context

Find the word *popular* in the passage. One definition below is a *synonym* for that word; it means the same or almost the same thing. One definition is an *antonym;* it has the opposite or nearly opposite meaning. The other has a completely different meaning. Label the definitions S for *synonym,* A for *antonym,* and D for *different.*

_____ a. common
_____ b. disliked
_____ c. favored

2. Distinguishing Fact from Opinion

Two of the statements below present *facts,* which can be proved correct. The other statement is an *opinion,* which expresses someone's thoughts or beliefs. Label the statements F for *fact* and O for *opinion.*

_____ a. In 1838 Angelina Grimké was the first woman to address a committee of the Massachusetts legislature on antislavery petitions.
_____ b. Sarah and Angelina Grimké were the daughters of a wealthy South Carolina slaveholder.

_____ c. Angelina Grimké was the most persuasive speaker of all the women involved in the antislavery movement.

3. Keeping Events in Order

Label the statements below 1, 2, and 3 to show the order in which the events happened.

_____ a. Angelina and Sarah Grimké joined the antislavery movement.

_____ b. The Grimké sisters moved north and became Quakers.

_____ c. The Grimké sisters joined the women's rights movement.

4. Making Correct Inferences

Two of the statements below are correct _inferences,_ or reasonable guesses. They are based on information in the passage. The other statement is an incorrect, or faulty, inference. Label the statements C for _correct_ inference and F for _faulty_ inference.

_____ a. If the Grimké sisters had not had personal experience with slavery, they would have been less persuasive.

_____ b. The Grimké sisters were influential in the battles against slavery and for women's rights.

_____ c. The Grimké sisters overcame their early upbringing to fight for what they knew was right.

5. Understanding Main Ideas

One of the statements below expresses the main idea of the passage. One statement is too general, or too broad. The other explains only part of the passage; it is too narrow. Label the statements M for _main idea,_ B for _too broad,_ and N for _too narrow._

_____ a. The Grimké sisters were active reformers in both the antislavery and women's rights movements.

_____ b. Sarah and Angelina Grimké became Quakers in order to join the antislavery movement.

_____ c. Quaker women made important contributions to many American social movements.

Correct Answers, Part A _____

Correct Answers, Part B _____

Total Correct Answers _____

The Speed of Light

On clear nights, stars from distant galaxies are easily observed by those on Earth because their light has traveled years through the vacuum of the universe. Light can travel through a vacuum, or empty space. A laboratory experiment demonstrates this: When air is pumped out of a glass vacuum chamber that contains a ringing bell, the bell remains visible while the sound fades away. A vacuum cannot transmit sound waves, but light rays continue to pass through it.

It is much easier to describe the interaction of light with matter than to explain light itself. One reason for this is that light cannot be seen until it interacts with matter. A beam of light is invisible unless it strikes an eye or unless there are particles that reflect parts of the beam to an eye. Also, light travels very fast. For centuries scientists disputed whether it required any time for light to move from one point to another.

The Renaissance scientist Galileo suggested one of the first experiments to measure the speed of light. Italian scientists carried out his idea. Two men were stationed on two hilltops. Each had a shaded lantern. The first man was to uncover his lantern. As soon as the second man saw the light, he was to uncover his lantern. The scientists tried to measure the time between the moment the first lantern was uncovered and the moment a return beam was detected. The speed of light was too fast to be measured in this way; therefore, the scientists concluded that light traveled instantaneously.

In 1675 Olaus Roemer, a Danish astronomer, was dealing with a different problem when he came across a method for measuring the speed of light. He was timing the eclipses of Jupiter's moons and noticed that the time between eclipses varied by several minutes. As Earth approached Jupiter, the time between eclipses grew shorter. As Earth receded from Jupiter, the time between eclipses grew longer. Roemer proposed that these discrepancies be used to calculate the time required for light to travel the diameter of Earth's orbit. Since the exact size of Earth's orbit was not yet known, and since Jupiter's irregular surface caused errors in timing the eclipses, he did not arrive at an accurate value for the speed of light. Still, Roemer had demonstrated that light took time to travel, but was too quick to measure with instruments then available.

Reading Time _____

Recalling Facts

1. Light cannot be seen until it
   - ❏ a. travels through a vacuum.
   - ❏ b. interacts with matter.
   - ❏ c. orbits Earth.

2. An experiment in which shaded lanterns were used to measure the speed of light was suggested by
   - ❏ a. a Dutch astronomer.
   - ❏ b. Italian scientists.
   - ❏ c. Galileo.

3. The shaded lantern experiment was a failure because
   - ❏ a. light travels instantaneously.
   - ❏ b. the speed of light is too fast to be measured that way.
   - ❏ c. of bad weather.

4. Olaus Roemer demonstrated that
   - ❏ a. Jupiter's surface is irregular.
   - ❏ b. light takes time to travel.
   - ❏ c. Earth's orbit creates light.

5. Light from stars
   - ❏ a. reaches Earth in seconds.
   - ❏ b. reaches Earth in hours.
   - ❏ c. takes years to travel to Earth.

Understanding Ideas

6. Early experiments to measure the speed of light were unsuccessful because
   - ❏ a. scientists lacked the proper instruments.
   - ❏ b. scientists did not know enough about light's characteristics.
   - ❏ c. light is invisible.

7. You can conclude from the article that the time between eclipses on Jupiter is affected by
   - ❏ a. the nearness of Earth.
   - ❏ b. Jupiter's irregular surface.
   - ❏ c. how it is measured.

8. You can conclude from the article that any sounds made by distant stars
   - ❏ a. would take years to travel to Earth.
   - ❏ b. would be translated into light rays in space.
   - ❏ c. would not be heard on Earth.

9. From the article you can conclude that for light from distant stars to be observed on Earth, it must
   - ❏ a. pass through a glass vacuum chamber.
   - ❏ b. interact with matter.
   - ❏ c. pass by the moons of Jupiter.

10. Neither Galileo nor Roemer was successful in measuring the speed of light, but
    - ❏ a. Roemer's results were more significant.
    - ❏ b. Galileo's results were more significant.
    - ❏ c. their methods were similar.

Staying Young at the Speed of Light

Even as a teenager, Albert Einstein was curious about the speed at which light travels. "What would the world look like if I rode on a beam of light?" he wrote. In 1921 Einstein was awarded the Nobel Prize in Physics for his work on the physics of light.

Einstein believed that the speed of light was the only constant physical property in the universe. This means that it always stays the same. Einstein's theory was that if the speed of light did not change, other physical properties had to. Time, for example, would pass more slowly in a spaceship traveling close to the speed of light compared to time passed on Earth. Imagine that one twin travels in space for 5 years at the speed of light while the other twin stays home. When the first twin returns, he will have aged 5 years—the time spent in space. The twin who stayed home, however, will have aged 10 years!

Einstein's theory about time was proved in 1977. Extremely accurate atomic clocks were placed aboard a satellite and sent into orbit. On their return, the clocks were compared with an atomic clock at the Naval Research Laboratory in Washington, D.C. The clocks that had gone into space had slowed down a tiny bit! Time had passed more slowly aboard the satellite.

1. **Recognizing Words in Context**

   Find the word *curious* in the passage. One definition below is a *synonym* for that word; it means the same or almost the same thing. One definition is an *antonym;* it has the opposite or nearly opposite meaning. The other has a completely different meaning. Label the definitions S for *synonym*, A for *antonym*, and D for *different*.

   _____ a. strange
   _____ b. interested
   _____ c. uninterested

2. **Distinguishing Fact from Opinion**

   Two of the statements below present *facts*, which can be proved correct. The other statement is an *opinion*, which expresses someone's thoughts or beliefs. Label the statements F for *fact* and O for *opinion*.

   _____ a. Time passes more slowly in a satellite than it does on Earth.
   _____ b. Einstein believed that the speed of light is constant.
   _____ c. Einstein was the most brilliant physicist of all time.

3. **Keeping Events in Order**

Two of the statements below describe events that happened at the same time. The other statement describes an event that happened before or after those events. Label them S for *same time,* B for *before,* or A for *after.*

_____ a. Einstein theorized that time passed more slowly the closer one came to the speed of light.

_____ b. Two atomic clocks orbited the earth in a satellite.

_____ c. A third atomic clock kept time at the Naval Research Laboratory.

4. **Making Correct Inferences**

Two of the statements below are correct *inferences,* or reasonable guesses. They are based on information in the passage. The other statement is an incorrect, or faulty, inference. Label the statements C for *correct* inference and F for *faulty* inference.

_____ a. If you travel close to the speed of light, you will never grow old.

_____ b. A person traveling in space, close to the speed of light, will age more slowly than a person on Earth.

_____ c. Scientists have been working to prove—or disprove—Einstein's theories.

5. **Understanding Main Ideas**

One of the statements below expresses the main idea of the passage. One statement is too general, or too broad. The other explains only part of the passage; it is too narrow. Label the statements M for *main idea,* B for *too broad,* and N for *too narrow.*

_____ a. To check Einstein's theory about time, atomic clocks were sent into space.

_____ b. Albert Einstein conceived a theory about the speed of light.

_____ c. Albert Einstein's theory about the relationship between time and the speed of light was proved by an experiment in 1977.

Correct Answers, Part A _____

Correct Answers, Part B _____

Total Correct Answers _____

The chief doorways of the world of international commerce are its harbors and ports. Through them pass cargoes and travelers from one part of the globe to another. A harbor is any sheltered body of water where boats or ships may moor or anchor. A port is an installation built around a harbor. It consists of facilities for loading and unloading vessels.

Ordinarily a harbor, either natural or artificial, must exist before a port facility can be set up. Some large harbors, such as San Francisco Bay on the California coast, for example, are used by several ports. Some ports, such as Chicago, Illinois, on Lake Michigan, are served by several small harbors.

The major requirements of a good harbor are direct access to the open water and sufficient depth for vessels to enter and exit safely. Ocean harbors are commonly 40 feet (12 meters) deep or more. The harbor should be well protected against storms and large waves. The bottom of the harbor should provide good holding ground for anchors; it must not be too rocky, too sandy, or too muddy. The harbor should also be spacious enough for ships to ride at anchor and to maneuver. Currents and tides must not be excessive.

Harbors are classified according to their location and structure. A natural coastal harbor is formed by a bay (New York City, for example) or by an offshore barrier such as an island (Hong Kong, China). A coastal breakwater harbor (Casablanca, Morocco) is sheltered by one or more artificial breakwaters. A tide gate harbor has locks that enclose areas of the harbor at high tide. As water leaves the harbor with low tide, the water level in the locked-off areas remains constant. At the port of Liverpool, England, tide gates are a necessity, for the tidal range of its harbor is approximately 21 feet (6.3 meters).

A natural river harbor (New Orleans, Louisiana) is sheltered from storms by the narrowness of the river. A river basin harbor (Rotterdam, the Netherlands) has slips—or docking ramps—dug into the riverbanks to accommodate vessels. A lake harbor or canal harbor (Brugge, Belgium) is on a small lake or an artificial canal that is connected with the open water by means of a navigable waterway. An open roadstead harbor offers little protection from storms, though it may serve as a port. These harbors are found along the coasts of Africa.

Reading Time _____

Recalling Facts

1. A sheltered body of water where boats may moor or anchor is called a
   - ❏ a. port.
   - ❏ b. harbor.
   - ❏ c. a breakwater.

2. New Orleans, Louisiana is an example of
   - ❏ a. a lake harbor.
   - ❏ b. an artificial canal.
   - ❏ c. a natural river harbor.

3. Loading and unloading of vessels takes place in a
   - ❏ a. port.
   - ❏ b. lock.
   - ❏ c. harbor.

4. A docking ramp for a boat or ship is called a
   - ❏ a. canal.
   - ❏ b. waterway.
   - ❏ c. slip.

5. In a good harbor,
   - ❏ a. there must be no currents and tides.
   - ❏ b. currents and tides must not be excessive.
   - ❏ c. boats should enter only at high tide.

Understanding Ideas

6. A harbor bottom that is too rocky, sandy, or muddy
   - ❏ a. is ideal for fish.
   - ❏ b. is probably artificial.
   - ❏ c. might result in a boat dragging its anchor.

7. You can conclude from the article that a breakwater
   - ❏ a. protects a harbor from breaking waves.
   - ❏ b. stops water from leaking.
   - ❏ c. separates lakes from the ocean.

8. A large, ocean-going vessel would probably unload its cargo
   - ❏ a. at an ocean harbor with an established port.
   - ❏ b. outside a harbor's breakwater.
   - ❏ c. in a lake harbor.

9. Tide gates with locks are necessary
   - ❏ a. where large ships anchor.
   - ❏ b. to maintain water levels in harbors with huge tidal ranges.
   - ❏ c. in most large harbors.

10. From the article you can conclude that a coastal breakwater harbor is
    - ❏ a. a sheltered harbor located on the coast.
    - ❏ b. probably at the mouth of a river.
    - ❏ c. protected by tide gates.

From its earliest days, Boston, like most other harbor cities, depended on the ocean to carry its sewage away. Boston's sewers and storm drains emptied right into harbor waters. As the Boston area grew, so did the sewage problems. By the early 1900s, Boston and 14 nearby cities were pumping their sewage into Boston harbor.

Boston officials built sewage treatment plants, but the problem grew faster than the solution. In the late 1960s, the treatment plants removed only about 10 percent of the pollutants. Barges carried waste out to sea and dumped it, only to have it come back to the harbor on the next tide.

By the early 1980s, many area beaches were closed. Fish and shellfish were no longer fit to eat. The harbor bottom was coated with slimy, gray goo. Then in 1982 the town of Quincy, miles to the south, sued Boston. They claimed that Quincy's harbor was dirty because Boston's harbor was dirty. The courts agreed.

Since then, innovative sewage treatment and disposal systems have been installed in the harbor. Treated waste is carried far out to sea, where it is disposed of safely. By the year 2000, Boston's harbor will be clean and safe.

1. **Recognizing Words in Context**

   Find the word *innovative* in the passage. One definition below is a *synonym* for that word; it means the same or almost the same thing. One definition is an *antonym;* it has the opposite or nearly opposite meaning. The other has a completely different meaning. Label the definitions S for *synonym,* A for *antonym,* and D for *different.*

   _____ a. time-tested
   _____ b. new
   _____ c. underground

2. **Distinguishing Fact from Opinion**

   Two of the statements below present *facts,* which can be proved correct. The other statement is an *opinion,* which expresses someone's thoughts or beliefs. Label the statements F for *fact* and O for *opinion.*

   _____ a. In the 1900s, Boston was pumping its sewage into the harbor waters.
   _____ b. Early sewage treatment plants removed only 10 percent of the pollutants.
   _____ c. By the year 2000, Boston Harbor will be clean and safe.

3. Keeping Events in Order

Label the statements below 1, 2, and 3 to show the order in which the events happened.

_____ a. The town of Quincy sued the city of Boston.

_____ b. New sewage disposal systems carry treated waste far out to sea.

_____ c. Boston pumped sewage directly into its harbor waters.

4. Making Correct Inferences

Two of the statements below are correct *inferences*, or reasonable guesses. They are based on information in the passage. The other statement is an incorrect, or faulty, inference. Label the statements C for *correct* inference and F for *faulty* inference.

_____ a. People once believed that pumping sewage into ocean waters was the best way to get rid of it.

_____ b. Boston never tried to keep its harbor clean.

_____ c. A court decision helped push Boston into finding solutions to its problem.

5. Understanding Main Ideas

One of the statements below expresses the main idea of the passage. One statement is too general, or too broad. The other explains only part of the passage; it is too narrow. Label the statements M for *main idea*, B for *too broad*, and N for *too narrow*.

_____ a. Pollution is a problem in harbors.

_____ b. Boston officials built treatment plants, but the plants could not keep up with the amount of sewage being produced.

_____ c. After centuries of pollution, Boston's harbor will be clean in the year 2000.

Correct Answers, Part A _____

Correct Answers, Part B _____

Total Correct Answers _____

　　　　Fire Extinguishers

Several types of fire extinguishers have been invented to put out different kinds of fires. They must be ready for instant use when fire breaks out. Most portable kinds operate for less than a minute, so they are useful only on small fires. The law requires ships, trains, intercity buses, and airplanes to carry extinguishers. They hang in schools, theaters, factories, stores, and high-rise buildings. Some people keep them in their homes, barns, and automobiles.

Since fuel, oxygen, and heat must be present in order for fire to exist, one or more of these three elements must be removed or reduced to extinguish a fire. If the heat is reduced by cooling the substance below the kindling temperature, the fire goes out. The cooling method is the most common way to put out a fire. Water is the best cooling agent because it is low in cost and usually readily available.

Another method of extinguishing fire is by eliminating or diluting the oxygen. This is usually done by smothering or blanketing the fire. A substance that is not readily combustible is used to cover the fire. Sand, foam, steam, or a nonflammable chemical may be employed. A blanket or rug may be used to cover and smother a small blaze.

A third method is called separation. This method involves removing the fuel, or combustible material, from a fire. In forest fires, for instance, the trees may be cut away leaving a fire lane in which the spreading flame can find no fuel. Explosives may be employed to block oil-well fires.

The method that is used to put out a fire depends upon the type of fire. Fires have been grouped in three classes. Fires in wood, paper, cloth, and similar common materials are called Class A fires. These materials usually form glowing coals, which help to sustain the fire. Such fires can be stopped most readily by cooling with water or watery solutions. Water has the advantage of usually being plentiful and cheap.

Blazes in flammable liquids such as gasoline, oil, or grease are called Class B fires. The material and the fire would float and spread if a stream of water were used on the flames. Such blazes are smothered; that is, oxygen from the air is cut off. Class C fires—those in charged electrical equipment— should be put out by an agent that does not conduct electricity.

Reading Time _____

Recalling Facts

1. The most common way to put out a fire is by
   - ❏ a. cooling.
   - ❏ b. diluting the oxygen.
   - ❏ c. removing the fuel.

2. The best cooling agent in putting out a fire is
   - ❏ a. a blanket.
   - ❏ b. gasoline.
   - ❏ c. water.

3. The method that is used to put out a fire depends upon
   - ❏ a. its location.
   - ❏ b. the type of fire.
   - ❏ c. the time of day.

4. A fire lane deprives a fire of
   - ❏ a. oxygen.
   - ❏ b. heat.
   - ❏ c. fuel.

5. Fires are grouped into
   - ❏ a. two classes.
   - ❏ b. three classes.
   - ❏ c. four classes.

Understanding Ideas

6. Large fires cannot be put out by portable fire extinguishers because the extinguishers
   - ❏ a. contain the wrong kind of chemicals.
   - ❏ b. do not contain enough chemicals.
   - ❏ c. often malfunction.

7. You can conclude from the article that sand
   - ❏ a. makes an excellent fuel.
   - ❏ b. does not burn easily.
   - ❏ c. is used in many fire extinguishers.

8. The cooling method is most often used to put out a fire, which suggests that most fires are
   - ❏ a. Class A fires.
   - ❏ b. Class B fires.
   - ❏ c. Class C fires.

9. The most important element in fighting a fire is
   - ❏ a. patience.
   - ❏ b. education.
   - ❏ c. speed.

10. Class A fires can be extinguished by
    - ❏ a. cooling only.
    - ❏ b. smothering only.
    - ❏ c. cooling, smothering, or removing the fuel.

Smoke Jumper

Jan stood in the plane's open doorway, holding tightly to the frame. Far below, a forest fire raged through a stand of pines. "Go!" shouted the team leader. Jan went, swiftly falling groundward. With a whoomp! her parachute blossomed above her. By tugging on the cords, Jan steered herself to a safe landing outside the fire zone. One by one, the other smoke jumpers on her team landed and unhooked themselves from their chutes.

The smoke jumpers worked hurriedly to clear a path around the fire. Armed with chainsaws, several began to fell dead trees. Their aim was to keep the fire contained. If they could keep it from spreading, it would be easier to put out.

"Jan! On your left!" Jan jumped to safety as a blazing pine tree crashed to the ground, showering white-hot sparks in all directions. "Thanks," she told her teammate.

Over the roar of the fire, the smoke jumpers heard the drone of an approaching plane. Flying low over the blaze, the air tanker began dumping its 1,400-gallon (6,370 liters) load of water. Beneath it, flames died out with a hiss and steam rose into the air. The smoke jumpers cheered and waved. Soon the ground crew would arrive with more firefighters and bull-dozers. Teamwork would keep this fire under control.

1. Recognizing Words in Context

Find the word *clear* in the passage. One definition below is a *synonym* for that word; it means the same or almost the same thing. One definition is an *antonym;* it has the opposite or nearly opposite meaning. The other has a completely different meaning. Label the definitions S for *synonym,* A for *antonym,* and D for *different.*

_____ a. transparent
_____ b. block
_____ c. empty

2. Distinguishing Fact from Opinion

Two of the statements below present *facts,* which can be proved correct. The other statement is an *opinion,* which expresses someone's thoughts or beliefs. Label the statements F for *fact* and O for *opinion.*

_____ a. The smoke jumpers tried to keep the fire contained.
_____ b. The air tanker dumped 1,400 gallons (6,370 liters) of water on the fire.
_____ c. Smoke jumping is the most dangerous profession in the world.

3. Keeping Events in Order

Two of the statements below describe events that happened at the same time. The other statement describes an event that happened before or after those events. Label them S for *same time*, B for *before*, or A for *after*.

_____ a. Someone yelled, "Jan! On your left!"

_____ b. A blazing pine tree crashed to the ground.

_____ c. Jan jumped to safety.

4. Making Correct Inferences

Two of the statements below are correct *inferences*, or reasonable guesses. They are based on information in the passage. The other statement is an incorrect, or faulty, inference. Label the statements C for *correct* inference and F for *faulty* inference.

_____ a. Smoke jumpers are firefighters who parachute into fire zones.

_____ b. Putting out forest fires is easy with teamwork.

_____ c. The first step in putting out a forest fire is containing the blaze.

5. Understanding Main Ideas

One of the statements below expresses the main idea of the passage. One statement is too general, or too broad. The other explains only part of the passage; it is too narrow. Label the statements M for *main idea*, B for *too broad*, and N for *too narrow*.

_____ a. An air tanker dumped water on the fire.

_____ b. Fighting forest fires requires the efforts of many people.

_____ c. A team of smoke jumpers parachuted into a fire zone and worked to contain the fire.

Correct Answers, Part A _____

Correct Answers, Part B _____

Total Correct Answers _____

Home, Sweet Home

Earth is a planet, a ball of matter, that orbits a star known as the Sun in a galaxy known as the Milky Way. Earth moves around the Sun in a regular orbit, as do the other planets in the solar system. Each planet has special characteristics. Some of these are well known to both scientists and the general public. Saturn, for example, is surrounded by a set of rings. Jupiter is famous as the largest planet in the solar system. Mars is known as the red planet, for the rusty red dust that covers its surface.

Earth also has special characteristics, and these are important to humans and other living things. All species on Earth contain carbon compounds and Earth is the only planet known to have the right temperature and atmosphere to support such life forms. This fact is so important that a special science called ecology has developed to address the interdependence of all living things and their environments. Ecologists try to find out how Earth's environments can be preserved so that living things will continue to survive on this planet.

Some scientists believe life forms may exist on millions of planets in the Milky Way. No one, however, can accurately predict the characteristics of such life forms. An indication of just how difficult such predictions are may be illustrated by the variety of life forms on Earth. Many millions of plants and animals have developed on this planet. Some thrive under conditions that are deadly for others. The range of Earth life suggests that forms of life quite different from any known on Earth might survive on planets with conditions that are uninhabitable for Earth species.

Many people believe that Earth is the only planet in the solar system that can support any kind of life. Scientists have theorized that some primitive forms of life may exist on the surface of Mars, but evidence gathered by missions to the Martian surface seems to indicate that this is unlikely.

Scientists at one time also believed that Venus might support life. Clouds hide the surface of Venus, so it was thought possible that the temperature and atmosphere on the planet's surface might be suitable for living things. It is now known, however, that the surface of Venus is too hot for liquid water to exist there. Life forms that humans are familiar with could not possibly live on Venus.

Reading Time _____

Recalling Facts

1. Earth is
   - ❏ a. the center of the solar system.
   - ❏ b. a carbon-based star.
   - ❏ c. a ball of matter orbiting the Sun.

2. The largest planet in the solar system is
   - ❏ a. Mars.
   - ❏ b. Saturn.
   - ❏ c. Jupiter.

3. The only planet known to have the right conditions to support carbon-based life is
   - ❏ a. Saturn.
   - ❏ b. Earth.
   - ❏ c. Mars.

4. The galaxy that contains the Sun is
   - ❏ a. the solar system.
   - ❏ b. the Milky Way.
   - ❏ c. the atmosphere.

5. Scientists who deal with the interdependence of living things are called
   - ❏ a. preservationists.
   - ❏ b. ecologists.
   - ❏ c. scientologists.

Understanding Ideas

6. The article states that the surface of Venus is too hot for liquid water, suggesting that
   - ❏ a. Earth species need liquid water to survive.
   - ❏ b. Earth is the only planet that can support life.
   - ❏ c. scientists don't know enough about Venus.

7. Scientific investigation into possible life forms in the solar system besides those on Earth suggests that
   - ❏ a. life definitely can be found on some other planet.
   - ❏ b. Earth is the only planet in the solar system that can support life.
   - ❏ c. life once existed on Mars.

8. You can conclude from the article that Earth's environment
   - ❏ a. is healthy.
   - ❏ b. is cause for concern among scientists.
   - ❏ c. cannot be preserved.

9. Whether other life forms can exist on other planets in the Milky Way galaxy is an issue
   - ❏ a. scientists agree on.
   - ❏ b. scientists disagree on.
   - ❏ c. of little interest among scientists.

10. It is likely that scientific investigation into finding other possible life forms
    - ❏ a. will continue.
    - ❏ b. is at an end.
    - ❏ c. will fail.

12   B   Home, Sweet Biosphere

On September 26, 1991, four women and four men entered a sealed structure to begin an unusual experiment. Its main purpose was to learn more about how our home—Earth—sustains itself by recycling water, air, and nutrients. Another purpose was to test ideas for building outposts on other planets, such as Mars.

The designers of Biosphere 2 (Earth being Biosphere 1) built a huge, glass-roofed structure covering 3.15 acres (1.26 hectares) of land. In separate areas within the structure were an Amazon-type rain forest, a desert, a saltwater marsh, and a 35-foot-deep (10.5 meter) "ocean" with its own coral reef and waves. Biosphere 2 was stocked with 3,800 species of plants and animals. There the bionauts, as the men and women were called, spent the next two years of their lives sealed off from the outside world.

There were good times and bad times for the bionauts. There were problems with foul air and failing crops. "It has not been easy looking at the same people over breakfast each day," said one. "A trip to Mars is going to be a lot harder—a much smaller space." What kept them going, they all agreed, was their focus on a goal: to create the world's first totally self-sustaining environment.

1. **Recognizing Words in Context**

    Find the word *separate* in the passage. One definition below is a *synonym* for that word; it means the same or almost the same thing. One definition is an *antonym;* it has the opposite or nearly opposite meaning. The other has a completely different meaning. Label the definitions S for *synonym*, A for *antonym,* and D for *different.*

    _____ a. distinct
    _____ b. severed
    _____ c. together

2. **Distinguishing Fact from Opinion**

    Two of the statements below present *facts,* which can be proved correct. The other statement is an *opinion,* which expresses someone's thoughts or beliefs. Label the statements F for *fact* and O for *opinion.*

    _____ a. A trip to Mars would be a lot harder than a stay in Biosphere 2.
    _____ b. The bionauts' stay began on September 26, 1991.
    _____ c. The bionauts lived in Biosphere 2 for two years.

3. Keeping Events in Order

Label the statements below 1, 2, and 3 to show the order in which the events happened.

_____ a. The bionauts entered Biosphere 2 and were sealed off from the world.

_____ b. Biosphere 2 was stocked with 3,800 species of plants and animals.

_____ c. The designers built a glass-roofed structure that covered 3.15 acres (1.26 hectares) of land.

4. Making Correct Inferences

Two of the statements below are correct *inferences,* or reasonable guesses. They are based on information in the passage. The other statement is an incorrect, or faulty, inference. Label the statements C for *correct* inference and F for *faulty* inference.

_____ a. The bionauts were dedicated to the success of the project.

_____ b. For their next project, the bionauts will go to Mars.

_____ c. Biosphere 2 helped scientists learn about Earth and its problems.

5. Understanding Main Ideas

One of the statements below expresses the main idea of the passage. One statement is too general, or too broad. The other explains only part of the passage; it is too narrow. Label the statements M for *main idea,* B for *too broad,* and N for *too narrow.*

_____ a. Biosphere 2 is just one step in finding out how people can live on another planet, such as Mars.

_____ b. For two years, eight people lived sealed inside Biosphere 2.

_____ c. Eight people lived for two years inside a sealed structure to study how Earth sustains itself.

Correct Answers, Part A _____

Correct Answers, Part B _____

Total Correct Answers _____

While studying to be a physician, W. Somerset Maugham wrote his first novel, *Liza of Lambeth*. Published in 1897, the year he completed his medical course, it is a story of life in the slums of London. The book's success determined Maugham's career. He never practiced medicine.

William Somerset Maugham was born on January 25, 1874, in Paris, France. His father was an English lawyer who was associated with the British Embassy in France. The boy's mother died when he was 8 and his father when he was 10. He was brought up by a childless uncle who was a clergyman in Kent, England. By the time he went to live with his uncle, young Maugham had read many books. Maugham attended King's School in Canterbury, Kent, then went to the University of Heidelberg in Germany. On returning to England he entered the medical school at St. Thomas' Hospital in London.

The young author wrote rapidly but very well. He drew his material largely from the life around him. His early works include a number of successful plays, and in 1908 he had four plays running in London at the same time.

Much of Maugham's philosophy is expressed in *Of Human Bondage,* a novel based largely on his own experiences. This book, which is generally considered to be his best work, brought him recognition as a serious literary artist. It is ranked among the great novels of the 20th century. The plot is drawn from Maugham's youth and young manhood. The literary characteristics of this book are detachment, coolness, irony, keen observation, and revelation of motives—all of which show his excellent craftsmanship. Among his other novels, one of the best-regarded is *The Moon and Sixpence.* Maugham patterned this book on the life of the French painter Paul Gauguin.

Maugham also wrote numerous short stories. One of the most famous of his short stories is "Rain." In his short stories as well as in his novels Maugham explains his philosophy of life. The chief elements of his philosophy are the unpredictability of human actions and reactions and one's bondage to one's emotions.

Maugham's later books include *The Razor's Edge,* a novel about a man's efforts to find peace in his soul, and *Then and Now,* a historical novel about Niccolo Machiavelli. *The Razor's Edge* and *Of Human Bondage* were adapted as motion pictures, as were some of Maugham's short stories.

Reading Time _____

Recalling Facts

1. Maugham studied
   - ❏ a. education.
   - ❏ b. medicine.
   - ❏ c. industry.

2. Maugham wrote about
   - ❏ a. the world of medicine.
   - ❏ b. the experiences of other writers.
   - ❏ c. the world around him.

3. Maugham's plays were
   - ❏ a. very successful.
   - ❏ b. failures.
   - ❏ c. seen on Broadway.

4. Maugham's best work is generally considered to be
   - ❏ a. *Of Human Bondage.*
   - ❏ b. an untitled book of philosophy.
   - ❏ c. *The Moon and Sixpence.*

5. Maugham wrote
   - ❏ a. magazine articles, novels, and movies.
   - ❏ b. medical journals.
   - ❏ c. novels, plays, and short stories.

Understanding Ideas

6. According to the article, Maugham should be considered
   - ❏ a. the greatest novelist of all time.
   - ❏ b. one of the greatest novelists of the 20th century.
   - ❏ c. a mediocre writer.

7. Maugham considered a person's emotions
   - ❏ a. a great blessing.
   - ❏ b. more important than intellect.
   - ❏ c. the source of many problems.

8. The article suggests that an important element in good writing is
   - ❏ a. portrayal of unpredictable emotions.
   - ❏ b. the ability to write from personal experience.
   - ❏ c. excellent craftsmanship.

9. Maugham believed that people respond to circumstances
   - ❏ a. in predictable ways.
   - ❏ b. in unpredictable ways.
   - ❏ c. by avoiding conflict.

10. Maugham was primarily a writer of
    - ❏ a. nonfiction.
    - ❏ b. fiction.
    - ❏ c. autobiography.

13　B　A Painter in Paradise

Painting was a passion for the great impressionist Eugène Henri Paul Gauguin (1848–1903). He could paint only in his spare time, however, while supporting his family with a job at the Paris stock exchange. Invitations to participate in the Fourth Impressionist Exhibition in 1879 and later in other art shows cost Gauguin his family but gave him the freedom to practice his art.

Gauguin was haunted by a dream of life elsewhere. He wrote to his estranged wife, "May the day come, and perhaps soon, when I can flee to the woods on a South Sea island, and live there in ecstasy, peace, and for art." A year later, Gauguin put his plan into action. He arrived in Tahiti in June 1891.

Gauguin returned to Paris in 1893 with magnificent paintings. In flat, strong colors and simple shapes, Gauguin depicted the Tahitian people and their landscape. Before his return to Europe, he wrote to a friend, "I have turned out 66 canvases of varying quality. . . . It is enough for one lone man."

Gauguin returned to the South Pacific in 1895, where he spent the rest of his life. Among the people drawn to the remote spots where Gauguin created his masterpieces was the author W. Somerset Maugham. Maugham's novel *The Moon and Sixpence* was based on the life of Gauguin.

1. **Recognizing Words in Context**

   Find the word *strong* in the passage. One definition below is a *synonym* for that word; it means the same or almost the same thing. One definition is an *antonym;* it has the opposite or nearly opposite meaning. The other has a completely different meaning. Label the definitions S for *synonym,* A for *antonym,* and D for *different.*

   _____ a. weak
   _____ b. powerful
   _____ c. firm

2. **Distinguishing Fact from Opinion**

   Two of the statements below present *facts,* which can be proved correct. The other statement is an *opinion,* which expresses someone's thoughts or beliefs. Label the statements F for *fact* and O for *opinion.*

   _____ a. Paul Gauguin was fortunate to be able to go to Tahiti.
   _____ b. Gauguin was invited to participate in several impressionist exhibitions.
   _____ c. Gauguin's travels in the South Pacific resulted in a large body of work.

3. Keeping Events in Order

Two of the statements below describe events that happened at the same time. The other statement describes an event that happened before or after those events. Label them S for *same time,* B for *before,* or A for *after.*

_____ a. Gauguin created many paintings of Tahitians and the Tahitian landscape.

_____ b. Gauguin worked at the Paris stock exchange.

_____ c. Gauguin painted in his spare time.

4. Making Correct Inferences

Two of the statements below are correct *inferences,* or reasonable guesses. They are based on information in the passage. The other statement is an incorrect, or faulty, inference. Label the statements C for *correct* inference and F for *faulty* inference.

_____ a. Gauguin was not happy with his life in Paris.

_____ b. His years in Tahiti gave Gauguin the freedom to devote himself to his painting.

_____ c. Gauguin's wife left him because he became a famous painter.

5. Understanding Main Ideas

One of the statements below expresses the main idea of the passage. One statement is too general, or too broad. The other explains only part of the passage; it is too narrow. Label the statements M for *main idea,* B for *too broad,* and N for *too narrow.*

_____ a. The impressionist painter Paul Gauguin found the freedom to paint in his years in the South Pacific.

_____ b. Paul Gauguin was a famous impressionist painter.

_____ c. Somerset Maugham's novel *The Moon and Sixpence* was based on the life of Gauguin.

Correct Answers, Part A _____

Correct Answers, Part B _____

Total Correct Answers _____

The Dairy Industry

Milk and milk products, such as butter, cheese, and ice cream, make up about an eighth of all the food eaten by the people of the United States. The annual production is about 140 billion pounds (63 billion kilograms). There are more than 300,000 farms with dairy cows in the United States, but only about 200,000 of these sell milk. The remainder use the milk as animal feed and for their own domestic consumption. There are about 150,000 people employed in the processing and delivery of dairy products throughout the United States.

Milk and milk products are processed and distributed to the public by dairy plants. The production of milk on dairy farms and the processing of milk and dairy products make up the dairy industry. Plants where butter and cheese or milk and cream are prepared for sale may also be called creameries or dairies.

The processing of dairy products begins on the farms that raise the milk cows. A typical dairy farm in the midwestern United States may have 60 cows, but a dairy farm in Florida or California may have 500 or more animals. Most milk in the United States is marketed through farmer-owned cooperatives. The milk that is produced on dairy farms is collected at county receiving stations for shipment to dairy plants.

Milk must be moved rapidly from the farm to the consumer and kept cold so that it will not spoil. On the dairy farm, milk is collected and quickly refrigerated in stainless steel bulk tanks. It is transported to the processing plant by refrigerated tank trucks where it is automatically pumped into holding tanks. It is then weighed, and samples are sent to the laboratory where tests are made for odor and flavor, bacteria, sediment, and milk protein and fat content. Milk of inferior quality may be rejected. Although dairy farms are routinely inspected by health officials, a farm from which any substandard milk came will be examined at once.

Milk is generally packaged in plastic containers or in cardboard cartons that are coated with paraffin wax to make them leak-proof. Filled containers then go to a refrigerated room to remain until the delivery trucks pick them up. Every day the equipment and all the machines through which the milk has flowed are sterilized. About one third of the labor time in a dairy plant may be spent in cleaning the equipment.

Reading Time _____

Recalling Facts

1. Most milk in the United States is marketed through
   - ❑ a. supermarkets.
   - ❑ b. farmer-owned cooperatives.
   - ❑ c. small food stores.

2. To keep it from spoiling, milk must be
   - ❑ a. bottled.
   - ❑ b. processed.
   - ❑ c. refrigerated.

3. Dairy farms are routinely inspected by
   - ❑ a. farmer-owned cooperatives.
   - ❑ b. health officials.
   - ❑ c. the Federal Bureau of Investigation.

4. Milk cartons made of cardboard are coated with paraffin wax so that they
   - ❑ a. are leak-proof.
   - ❑ b. are sterilized.
   - ❑ c. can be inspected.

5. The number of farms with dairy cows in the United States is
   - ❑ a. about 100.
   - ❑ b. about 500.
   - ❑ c. more than 300,000.

Understanding Ideas

6. It is likely that plants that produce milk also
   - ❑ a. raise cows.
   - ❑ b. produce meat.
   - ❑ c. produce milk products.

7. You can conclude from the article that dairy farming in Florida and California is
   - ❑ a. not very profitable.
   - ❑ b. a major industry.
   - ❑ c. the most important industry.

8. You can conclude from the article that milk sold in stores
   - ❑ a. has been inspected.
   - ❑ b. has been processed in California or Florida.
   - ❑ c. comes from the Midwest.

9. You can conclude from the article that milk must meet standards for
   - ❑ a. protein and fat content.
   - ❑ b. calories.
   - ❑ c. sugar content.

10. A major concern in processing milk is
   - ❑ a. cleanliness.
   - ❑ b. delivery.
   - ❑ c. leakage.

She had roles in two movies, ate a gossip columnist's hat, has a star on Hollywood Boulevard, and toured the country in her own railroad car. Who was she? She was a seven-year-old Jersey cow who became known to the world as Elsie, the Borden Cow.

Born in 1932 on a dairy farm in Brookfield, Massachusetts, Elsie—then named You'll Do Lobelia—lived a normal cow life until 1939. At that time, the symbol of Borden's Milk was a popular cartoon cow named Elsie. Borden's staff at the 1939 World's Fair found that the question most people asked was, "Where's Elsie?" Company officials decided that if the public wanted a real Elsie, they should have one. They chose the best-looking cow in the barns—You'll Do Lobelia.

By the time the fair ended, more than seven million people had come to see Lobelia—now called Elsie. In July 1940, RKO Pictures offered her the starring role of Buttercup in a film of Louisa May Alcott's *Little Men*. So Elsie went to Hollywood. More than 12,000 newspaper stories appeared about her trip.

Then disaster struck in April 1941. Badly injured in a truck accident, Elsie died 10 days later. Millions mourned her. Today, the farm where Elsie was born is a wildlife sanctuary.

1. **Recognizing Words in Context**

Find the word *real* in the passage. One definition below is a *synonym* for that word; it means the same or almost the same thing. One definition is an *antonym*; it has the opposite or nearly opposite meaning. The other has a completely different meaning. Label the definitions S for *synonym*, A for *antonym*, and D for *different*.

_____ a. artificial
_____ b. essential
_____ c. genuine

2. **Distinguishing Fact from Opinion**

Two of the statements below present *facts*, which can be proved correct. The other statement is an *opinion*, which expresses someone's thoughts or beliefs. Label the statements F for *fact* and O for *opinion*.

_____ a. More than seven million people visited Elsie at the 1939 World's Fair.
_____ b. Elsie was the best-looking cow in the barns.
_____ c. Millions mourned Elsie when she died.

3. Keeping Events in Order

Label the statements below 1, 2, and 3 to show the order in which the events happened.

_____ a. Visitors to the 1939 World's Fair kept asking where Elsie was.

_____ b. Elsie starred in a movie of *Little Men*.

_____ c. Borden's Milk officials chose You'll Do Lobelia to become Elsie, the Borden Cow.

4. Making Correct Inferences

Two of the statements below are correct *inferences*, or reasonable guesses. They are based on information in the passage. The other statement is an incorrect, or faulty, inference. Label the statements C for *correct* inference and F for *faulty* inference.

_____ a. Elsie was a popular public figure.

_____ b. People were fascinated with the symbol of Borden's Milk.

_____ c. Cows make good movie stars.

5. Understanding Main Ideas

One of the statements below expresses the main idea of the passage. One statement is too general, or too broad. The other explains only part of the passage; it is too narrow. Label the statements M for *main idea*, B for *too broad*, and N for *too narrow*.

_____ a. Animals are popular advertising symbols.

_____ b. Elsie, the Borden Cow, became a popular public figure.

_____ c. Elsie has a star on Hollywood Boulevard.

Correct Answers, Part A _____

Correct Answers, Part B _____

Total Correct Answers _____

A bicycle, or bike, is a simple machine. Basically, a bike consists of two wheels housed in a frame. It includes a steering mechanism, a seat, and two pedals. This simple machine provides recreation and exercise, as well as fuel-efficient transportation to people around the globe. In some countries, such as China, bicycles are as important as autos are in the United States. Bike racing ranks behind only soccer as a popular sport in Europe and Latin America.

Every year throughout the world an increasing number of people buy bicycles. In the early 1980s about 9 million bikes were sold annually in the United States. China, however, is a much larger producer of bikes than the United States.

Historians do not know who invented the bicycle. Leonardo da Vinci, the well-known Italian artist of the 15th century, drew some rough sketches of something resembling a bike. In 1690, a French inventor named De Sivrac built a hobbyhorse that had wheels but no pedals. It moved by means of the action of the rider's feet pushing against the ground.

Bicycle development took a major step about 1840. A Scottish black-smith, Kirkpatrick Macmillan, built a device with two pedals, connected by a rod, that provided power to the rear wheel. Following Macmillan's invention, the bicycle became a popular and inexpensive means of transportation in England, France, and the United States. The roads were full of ruts and holes, but the development of a bicycle called the "ordinary" helped solve this problem. An ordinary had an enormous front wheel that measured as high as 5 feet (about 150 centimeters) or more. The large wheel enabled the rider to cruise easily over rough terrain; however, the great height of the ordinary made it difficult to mount and ride. An accident could cause serious injury.

Bicycle riding became safer in 1886 with the appearance of the safety bike, which had two wheels of equal size. Pedals drove the rear wheel by means of a chain and sprockets. In 1888 John Dunlop of Scotland invented a pneumatic, or air-filled, tire that made bike riding much smoother.

The next improvement came about 1900 when an English manufacturer developed a three-speed wheel hub for bicycles. This enabled riders to cover hilly terrain at higher speeds. In the 1960s the ten-speed gearshift became common on bikes, though many still have a three-speed system or no gearshift at all.

Reading Time _____

Recalling Facts

1. The inventor of the bicycle is
   - ❑ a. Leonardo da Vinci.
   - ❑ b. Kirkpatrick Macmillan.
   - ❑ c. unknown.

2. In Europe and Latin America, bike racing is
   - ❑ a. the most popular sport.
   - ❑ b. the second most popular sport.
   - ❑ c. less popular than in America.

3. An early bicycle with an enormous front wheel was called
   - ❑ a. a cruiser.
   - ❑ b. an ordinary.
   - ❑ c. a tricycle.

4. Bike riding became much smoother with the invention of
   - ❑ a. a chain and sprockets.
   - ❑ b. equal-size wheels.
   - ❑ c. a pneumatic tire.

5. As a producer of bikes, China ranks
   - ❑ a. ahead of the United States.
   - ❑ b. behind the United States.
   - ❑ c. the same as the United States.

Understanding Ideas

6. One advantage a bicycle has over a car for transportation is its
   - ❑ a. lightweight frame.
   - ❑ b. fuel efficiency.
   - ❑ c. safety features.

7. You can conclude from the article that bicycles are important in China because
   - ❑ a. bikes are more affordable than cars.
   - ❑ b. the terrain is hilly.
   - ❑ c. many bikes are produced there.

8. One of the biggest challenges facing early bicyclists was
   - ❑ a. safety on rough terrain.
   - ❑ b. the cost of fuel.
   - ❑ c. seat height.

9. You can conclude from the article that the ability to change speeds gives a bicyclist
   - ❑ a. more control.
   - ❑ b. less control.
   - ❑ c. increased fuel efficiency.

10. Today's bicycles are powered by
    - ❑ a. the action of the rider's feet against the ground.
    - ❑ b. the movement of pedals pushed by the rider.
    - ❑ c. compressed air in the tires.

The Father of the Bicycle Industry

James Starley (1830–1881) began his career in England's Coventry Machinist's Company, building velocipedes. *Velocipede* is an early term for a lightweight wheeled vehicle propelled by a rider—a cycle. Starley soon founded Starley Brothers Ltd., from which would come many innovative cycle designs. In 1871 Starley built the first bicycle with metal-spoked wheels. Soon after, a rival company came out with tension wheels, provoking what came to be called "the battle of the wheel." Starley improved his original wheel with the cross-spoke design that remains the basis of bicycle wheels today.

Starley was always trying to make better cycles. He was the first to use sprockets, cogs, and chains in cycles. When one of his two-person cycles dumped him in a patch of nettles, he revised the gears to allow the drive wheels to turn independently, the first use in a cycle of a differential gear. He also pioneered the use of hollow-frame tubing to make cycles lighter and more maneuverable.

After Starley's death, his sons carried on his work, producing a complete line of bicycles, tricycles, and "sociables," multiwheel vehicles for more than one rider. In the 1880s Starley's nephew, John Starley, designed the first safety bicycle, beginning a new era of bicycle building.

1. **Recognizing Words in Context**

   Find the word *innovative* in the passage. One definition below is a *synonym* for that word; it means the same or almost the same thing. One definition is an *antonym;* it has the opposite or nearly opposite meaning. The other has a completely different meaning. Label the definitions S for *synonym,* A for *antonym,* and D for *different.*

   _____ a. regressive
   _____ b. deliberate
   _____ c. progressive

2. **Distinguishing Fact from Opinion**

   Two of the statements below present *facts,* which can be proved correct. The other statement is an *opinion,* which expresses someone's thoughts or beliefs. Label the statements F for *fact* and O for *opinion.*

   _____ a. James Starley built the first metal-spoke bicycle wheels.
   _____ b. John Starley designed the first safety bicycle.
   _____ c. Starley was always trying to make better cycles.

3. **Keeping Events in Order**

   Label the statements below 1, 2, and 3 to show the order in which the events happened.

   _____ a. James Starley put differential gears in a cycle.

   _____ b. James Starley designed the cross-spoke wheel.

   _____ c. John Starley designed the safety bicycle.

4. **Making Correct Inferences**

   Two of the statements below are correct *inferences*, or reasonable guesses. They are based on information in the passage. The other statement is an incorrect, or faulty, inference. Label the statements C for *correct* inference and F for *faulty* inference.

   _____ a. James Starley had a key role in developing the bicycle.

   _____ b. Most of the cycle design advances from Starley's company came after Starley's death.

   _____ c. Starley's work influenced others in the bicycle field.

5. **Understanding Main Ideas**

   One of the statements below expresses the main idea of the passage. One statement is too general, or too broad. The other explains only part of the passage; it is too narrow. Label the statements M for *main idea*, B for *too broad*, and N for *too narrow*.

   _____ a. The bicycle has been through many changes.

   _____ b. James Starley was the first to use sprockets, cogs, and chains to drive bicycle wheels.

   _____ c. James Starley made changes in bicycle design that are in use in today's bicycles.

Correct Answers, Part A _____

Correct Answers, Part B _____

Total Correct Answers _____

Animals of Africa

Africa is home to some of the largest and most varied wildlife in the world—from the rare mountain gorillas in the highlands of Rwanda and Zaire to the lemurs of Madagascar. In the past 50 years, however, the wildlife of Africa has been greatly reduced. In the savanna regions there were once vast herds of zebras, wildebeest, and antelopes. With them were their predators: the lions, cheetahs, and leopards. Other large-animal populations included the hyenas, jackals, rhinoceroses, hippopotamuses, and elephants. The numbers of these animals and others are dwindling, partly as a result of overhunting and poaching and partly because large areas of their natural habitats have been taken over for farming.

Many species are in such danger that they are threatened with extinction. To protect wildlife, several countries have set aside land for the exclusive use of wild animals. These areas, called national parks, have tourist facilities that permit visitors to watch the animals in a natural setting. The parks also make it possible for scientists to study animal behavior in the wild.

Although scientists, tourists, and animal lovers praise the national parks, creation of these areas has led to conflict with people who want to use the land for other purposes. The population of Africa is growing rapidly and there is a shortage of land for raising domestic animals. People often associate Africa with big game, yet there are far more farm animals in Africa than there are wild ones. The cattle, poultry, goats, and pigs that are raised for food compete with the wild animals for living space and grazing lands. The parks are blamed for depriving herders and farmers of land.

In addition to the conflict between the national parks and the herders and farmers, there are other conflicts addressing how people and animals live together in Africa. The tsetse fly, which transmits sleeping sickness, has made large tracts of land in East and Central Africa uninhabitable for people or cattle. The Anopheles mosquito is a carrier of malaria and other diseases. Rodents eat grain and can carry diseases, such as cholera. Even the beautiful birds of Africa can be destructive to grain crops.

Not all animals are in conflict with people in Africa; some are very helpful. One common ant in the southern part of Africa builds high anthills. The clay mud from these anthills is ideal for making bricks for houses and farm buildings.

Reading Time _____

Recalling Facts

1. In the past 50 years the wildlife of Africa has
   - ❑ a. greatly increased.
   - ❑ b. been greatly reduced.
   - ❑ c. been tamed.

2. African animals are threatened with extinction due to
   - ❑ a. parks and tourism.
   - ❑ b. hunting, poaching, and loss of habitat.
   - ❑ c. climate changes.

3. The greatest number of animals in Africa are
   - ❑ a. big game animals.
   - ❑ b. birds.
   - ❑ c. domestic farm animals.

4. A carrier of malaria and other diseases is the
   - ❑ a. African ant.
   - ❑ b. tsetse fly.
   - ❑ c. Anopheles mosquito.

5. African birds are a problem because they
   - ❑ a. kill big game.
   - ❑ b. carry diseases.
   - ❑ c. destroy grain crops.

Understanding Ideas

6. The land conflict between people and animals in Africa
   - ❑ a. should be resolved in favor of animals.
   - ❑ b. should be resolved in favor of people.
   - ❑ c. is difficult to resolve.

7. The main advantage of national parks is that
   - ❑ a. tourism is promoted.
   - ❑ b. animals are protected.
   - ❑ c. scientists can study animals in the wild.

8. Land for raising domestic animals in Africa is important because these animals
   - ❑ a. are a source of food for a growing population.
   - ❑ b. take up less space than wild animals.
   - ❑ c. provide enjoyment for tourists.

9. The article points out that
   - ❑ a. there is no easy answer to Africa's animal problems.
   - ❑ b. Africa's animal problems are the result of poor management.
   - ❑ c. the major problem facing Africa today is disease-carrying animals.

10. You can conclude from the article that
    - ❑ a. hunting is no longer allowed in Africa.
    - ❑ b. animals threatened with extinction can be saved.
    - ❑ c. the extinction of wild game in Africa is inevitable.

16 | B | Portrait of a Lion

Inga and I were on assignment in Africa to write and photograph a magazine article on lions. After a long day of missed shots, we were rolling back to camp in our open car, tired and hot. Then Inga spotted a lioness in an acacia tree. The lioness was stretched out asleep on a limb just 10 feet (3 meters) above the road.

"I'll snap her picture as we pass underneath," Inga said.

As the car passed beneath her, the lioness woke up and scowled down at us. "I missed the shot," said Inga. "Let's go around again." So we did, again and then a third time. By now the lioness was crouched, hindquarters high, front paws gathered under her chest. The black tuft on her heavy tail thumped on the bark. "She won't jump," Inga assured me as we came closer.

"Don't be so sure!" I snapped. Just as we reached the tree, the lioness snarled loudly. My foot left the gas, but the car stalled, directly under the big cat! Her whiskers and my face were less than a lion's length apart. Waiting for the cat to explode from the tree, I frantically tried to restart the engine. Inga kept shooting pictures. The heavy smell of lion was in my nose as the car came to life.

"These shots will be fantastic!" Inga cried as we drove on.

1. Recognizing Words in Context

Find the word *cried* in the passage. One definition below is a *synonym* for that word; it means the same or almost the same thing. One definition is an *antonym*; it has the opposite or nearly opposite meaning. The other has a completely different meaning. Label the definitions S for *synonym*, A for *antonym*, and D for *different*.

_____ a. wept
_____ b. shouted
_____ c. whispered

2. Distinguishing Fact from Opinion

Two of the statements below present *facts*, which can be proved correct. The other statement is an *opinion*, which expresses someone's thoughts or beliefs. Label the statements F for *fact* and O for *opinion*.

_____ a. The narrator and Inga were in Africa to do an article on lions.
_____ b. The shots Inga got of the lioness were going to be fantastic.
_____ c. A lioness was sleeping on a limb of an acacia tree.

3. Keeping Events in Order

Two of the statements below describe events that happened at the same time. The other statement describes an event that happened before or after those events. Label them S for *same time,* B for *before,* and A for *after.*

_____ a. The narrator tried to restart the car.

_____ b. The lioness snarled.

_____ c. Inga kept snapping pictures.

4. Making Correct Inferences

Two of the statements below are correct *inferences,* or reasonable guesses. They are based on information in the passage. The other statement is an incorrect, or faulty, inference. Label the statements C for *correct* inference and F for *faulty* inference.

_____ a. Inga was more concerned about getting a good picture than with their safety.

_____ b. The lioness was preparing to attack the people in the car.

_____ c. The lioness was just bluffing.

5. Understanding Main Ideas

One of the statements below expresses the main idea of the passage. One statement is too general, or too broad. The other explains only part of the passage; it is too narrow. Label the statements M for *main idea,* B for *too broad,* and N for *too narrow.*

_____ a. The car stalled when the lioness snarled.

_____ b. The narrator and a photographer risked their lives to get photographs of a lioness in a tree.

_____ c. Reporters and photographers sometimes do stories on wild animals.

Correct Answers, Part A _____

Correct Answers, Part B _____

Total Correct Answers _____

The Making of a Jet

The research, design, and production of airplanes, missiles, and spacecraft make up the aerospace industry. It is a relatively young industry, less than a century old. Its birthplace was the bicycle shop of Orville and Wilbur Wright in Dayton, Ohio. They built the first successful airplane, which they tested in December 1903. Today an aerospace manufacturing plant resembles a small city. Its offices, warehouses, factories, and other buildings may stretch for blocks.

A jet airplane has many thousands of parts. It therefore takes at least four or five years to start, develop, and produce one. Research and development, including engineering and testing, take place before manufacturing. Military or business leaders first specify the characteristics of the vehicle they want built. In a military plane fast takeoff, supersonic speed, armament, and bomb load are important. In a commercial airliner the number of passengers and cargo weight come first. Manufacturers of aerospace vehicles often develop their own designs.

The engineering department may have a thousand specialists. They prepare drawings that show the general outlines of the vehicle. Scale models are made for testing in a wind tunnel. Next a full-sized mock-up is built. Draftsmen then draw blueprints; a medium-sized jet plane may require up to 18,000 blueprints. Finally, an experimental model, or prototype, is constructed. Test pilots prove its airworthiness in actual flight.

The production of the vehicle takes careful planning. Plant layout experts make a miniature scale model of the plant to solve production problems. Contracts are let to subcontractors who will supply the parts. Workers must be trained. Machines, tools, fixtures, and jigs are ordered. Fixtures are devices for holding parts during machining or assembly. A jig is a device for guiding a tool, such as a drill. Metal parts are anodized to give them a tough, thin film that prevents corrosion and bonds paint. They are heat-treated to make them stronger and sprayed with paint to protect them.

When production begins, the factory is noisy and busy. Workers use riveting guns, mechanical hammers, saws, and many other tools. Overhead cranes carry materials. Tractors, trailers, and lift trucks move supplies.

The aerospace industry has borrowed the assembly-line method from the automobile makers. As the vehicle moves down the line, assemblers, riveters, and welders fit sections to it—the nose, fuselage, wings, tail, engines, and so on—until the craft is completed and ready for its test flight.

Reading Time _____

Recalling Facts

1. The aerospace industry
   - ❑ a. began during Roman times.
   - ❑ b. is less than 100 years old.
   - ❑ c. is 200 years old.

2. The first successful airplane was built
   - ❑ a. by the Orville brothers.
   - ❑ b. in Colorado.
   - ❑ c. by the Wright brothers.

3. After a mock-up of an airplane is built,
   - ❑ a. pilots test the vehicle.
   - ❑ b. various designs are considered.
   - ❑ c. draftsmen draw blueprints.

4. Airplanes are put together
   - ❑ a. one at a time.
   - ❑ b. on an assembly line.
   - ❑ c. by computers.

5. To prevent corrosion, metal parts are
   - ❑ a. painted.
   - ❑ b. heat-treated.
   - ❑ c. anodized.

Understanding Ideas

6. The article wants you to understand that the making of a jet
   - ❑ a. requires a small, but well-organized team.
   - ❑ b. requires years of detailed planning, development, and production.
   - ❑ c. is primarily the responsibility of engineers.

7. You can conclude from the article that military and passenger aircraft
   - ❑ a. are essentially built from the same designs.
   - ❑ b. are designed to suit the special needs of each type of craft.
   - ❑ c. have similar characteristics.

8. You can conclude from the article that the assembly-line method of airplane production is
   - ❑ a. the most efficient and cost-effective method.
   - ❑ b. the safest way.
   - ❑ c. more suitable for producing cars than airplanes.

9. It is likely that drawings and models of airplanes to be built serve to
   - ❑ a. solve problems at the earliest possible stages.
   - ❑ b. provide more jobs for researchers.
   - ❑ c. increase production speed on the assembly line.

10. Test-flying is important because
    - ❑ a. possible mistakes in design or production can be discovered.
    - ❑ b. an airplane is only as good as the pilot who flies it.
    - ❑ c. safety standards must be met.

Jet pilot Judy Campbell began flying at 17 and had her instructor's license by the time she was 20. The daughter of a US Air pilot, Campbell seemed destined to fly.

After she graduated from college, Campbell joined the United States Air Force. She didn't much enjoy officer training—"You're not treated well," she says. "Their sole intent is to turn you into a military officer in three months." Flight training, on the other hand, was a totally different experience—especially formation flying. "At 500 miles [805 kilometers] an hour, you're only 20 inches [50.8 centimeters] away from the planes you're flying beside, wingtip to wingtip. Very exciting," Campbell reports.

After two years in the air force, Campbell joined TWA. When the Gulf War erupted, Campbell was called back into the service. Her job—flying a C–141 cargo plane to Saudi Arabia. Because of the danger, Campbell had to wear chemical warfare gear—a heavy rubber suit—over her flight suit.

Today, as a first officer flying B–727s for Federal Express, Campbell flies less dangerous missions. As for crises, she remarks, "We train so much to fly with engines out that when something happens in real life, it's no big deal."

1. **Recognizing Words in Context**

Find the word *sole* in the passage. One definition below is a *synonym* for that word; it means the same or almost the same thing. One definition is an *antonym*; it has the opposite or nearly opposite meaning. The other has a completely different meaning. Label the definitions S for *synonym*, A for *antonym*, and D for *different*.

_____ a. single
_____ b. fish
_____ c. multiple

2. **Distinguishing Fact from Opinion**

Two of the statements below present *facts*, which can be proved correct. The other statement is an *opinion*, which expresses someone's thoughts or beliefs. Label the statements F for *fact* and O for *opinion*.

_____ a. Pilots in training are not treated well by the United States Air Force.
_____ b. Judy Campbell spent two years in the Air Force.
_____ c. During the Gulf War, pilots wore chemical warfare gear.

3. Keeping Events in Order

Two of the statements below describe events that happened at the same time. The other statement describes an event that happened before or after those events. Label them S for *same time*, B for *before*, and A for *after*.

_____ a. Judy Campbell joined the United States Air Force.

_____ b. Campbell flew her plane wingtip to wingtip with other planes.

_____ c. Campbell's plane was going 500 miles (805 kilometers) an hour.

4. Making Correct Inferences

Two of the statements below are correct *inferences*, or reasonable guesses. They are based on information in the passage. The other statement is an incorrect, or faulty, inference. Label the statements C for *correct* inference and F for *faulty* inference.

_____ a. From an early age, Judy Campbell wanted to fly.

_____ b. Campbell has never been afraid while flying.

_____ c. Judy Campbell has had a great deal of experience as a pilot.

5. Understanding Main Ideas

One of the statements below expresses the main idea of the passage. One statement is too general, or too broad. The other explains only part of the passage; it is too narrow. Label the statements M for *main idea*, B for *too broad*, and N for *too narrow*.

_____ a. Pilot Judy Campbell has had a wide variety of experience as a pilot.

_____ b. Judy Campbell flew a cargo plane during the Gulf War.

_____ c. Women pilots fly for commercial airlines.

Correct Answers, Part A _____

Correct Answers, Part B _____

Total Correct Answers _____

The great structures of ancient Egypt and Greece and roads built by the Romans show that humans have been skilled at quarrying for thousands of years. Quarrying is primarily the mining of nonmetallic rock from shallow, open-pit mines called quarries. The two major products of quarrying are dimension-stone blocks or slabs of such material as limestone, granite, marble, or sandstone—and crushed stone. The great pyramids in Egypt, constructed more than 4,500 years ago, provide evidence of early building with quarried stone. Blocks of limestone weighing as much as 16 tons (16.3 tonnes) were quarried and transported long distances to pyramid sites.

Older quarrying methods were almost always concerned with obtaining dimension stone for use as building material. Hence, quarrying was limited to areas in which rock of uniform texture and coloration was available. This was usually granite or limestone.

All three major types of rock are quarried: igneous, metamorphic, and sedimentary. The most commonly quarried igneous rock is granite. Marble, quartzite, and slate are the metamorphic rocks most frequently quarried. Sedimentary rocks that are quarried include sandstone and shale. Limestone, marble, and granite are still much used for buildings and monuments. Slate is used for roofing and quartzite for flagging. Crushed stone is used for concrete and road building. Limestone is used in the operation of blast furnaces.

Quarrying technique involves deep drilling and blasting to break the rock. When usable rock is found, the surface is cleared. A cut, or channel, is made to separate the rock from the solid bed, or mass. Large blocks are separated from the parent mass, sometimes with the use of low-powered explosives. High-energy explosives that would shatter the rock cannot be used for dimension stone. A single blast may produce as much as 20,000 tons (20,400 tonnes) of broken stone. The broken stone is crushed into smaller pieces that are separated into uniform classes by screening methods.

For most dimension-stone quarrying, success depends largely on taking advantage of joints and cleavage plates, or breaks, in the rock. Granite, for example, has a rift along which it may be split with relative ease. For softer rocks, such as limestone and sandstone, a channeling machine is used. This is a power-driven cutter that makes a slot about two inches (five centimeters) wide and several feet or meters deep. Drilling closely spaced holes and cutting away rock in between may channel harder rock, such as granite.

Reading Time _____

Recalling Facts

1. Quarries are
   - ❏ a. nonmetallic rocks.
   - ❏ b. shallow, open-pit mines.
   - ❏ c. crushed stones.

2. The most commonly quarried igneous rock is
   - ❏ a. granite.
   - ❏ b. marble.
   - ❏ c. slate.

3. The ancient Egyptian pyramids were constructed of
   - ❏ a. slabs.
   - ❏ b. dimension-stone blocks.
   - ❏ c. crushed stone.

4. The three major types of rock are
   - ❏ a. marble, quartz, and slate.
   - ❏ b. quarried, monumental, and block.
   - ❏ c. igneous, metamorphic, and sedimentary.

5. The success of dimension-stone quarrying depends on
   - ❏ a. the quality of explosive used.
   - ❏ b. how much workers are paid.
   - ❏ c. taking advantage of breaks in the rock.

Understanding Ideas

6. For a project requiring stone that will withstand the punishment of time and weather, the most suitable rock to use is probably
   - ❏ a. sandstone.
   - ❏ b. limestone.
   - ❏ c. granite.

7. The article suggests that ancient Greeks and Romans
   - ❏ a. were master builders.
   - ❏ b. knew little about quarrying.
   - ❏ c. competed against each other.

8. Successful quarrying today
   - ❏ a. depends on technology.
   - ❏ b. uses outdated methods.
   - ❏ c. is subject to the weather.

9. Over the centuries, stone has been used for building most likely because
   - ❏ a. trees have always been scarce.
   - ❏ b. it is hard to work with.
   - ❏ c. it is durable and available.

10. The article wants you to understand that quarrying
    - ❏ a. requires patience and skill.
    - ❏ b. takes place near bodies of water.
    - ❏ c. is only one of many methods used to obtain stone for building.

Quarrying for the Pyramids

Building the great pyramids of Egypt was a heroic undertaking. Workers cut rock with simple copper and stone tools. They moved massive blocks into place with muscle power alone, since the Egyptians did not know the principle of the block and tackle.

Thousands of workers, organized into teams, labored in the quarries. To obtain relatively soft limestone, tunnels were dug into the face of cliffs from which huge caverns were cut, block by block. Rock columns were left to support the roofs.

Granite is so hard that the Egyptians' copper chisels could hardly make a dent in it. Special hammers of a very hard stone called dolomite were used to chip rough gutters, or slots, in quarry walls. Workers fitted wooden wedges into the slots and soaked them with water. The wet wood expanded, splitting off massive chunks of rock that were then hammered into rough blocks.

The blocks were painted with a variety of quarry marks. Some marks indicated the blocks' destination. Others cautioned, "This side up." Still others gave the name of the quarry gang that carved them. The gangs' names showed the workers' pride in their efforts: "Vigorous Gang" and "Enduring Gang" are two examples.

1. Recognizing Words in Context

Find the word *gang* in the passage. One definition below is a *synonym* for that word; it means the same or almost the same thing. One definition is an *antonym;* it has the opposite or nearly opposite meaning. The other has a completely different meaning. Label the definitions S for *synonym,* A for *antonym,* and D for *different.*

_____ a. individual
_____ b. team
_____ c. hoodlums

2. Distinguishing Fact from Opinion

Two of the statements below present *facts,* which can be proved correct. The other statement is an *opinion,* which expresses someone's thoughts or beliefs. Label the statements F for *fact* and O for *opinion.*

_____ a. Building the great pyramids of Egypt was a heroic undertaking.
_____ b. The Egyptians did not know the principle of the block and tackle.
_____ c. The blocks were painted with a variety of quarry marks.

3. **Keeping Events in Order**

   Label the statements below 1, 2, and 3 to show the order in which the events happened.

   _____ a. Workers fitted wooden wedges into the slots and soaked them with water.

   _____ b. Workers chipped rough gutters in the quarry walls.

   _____ c. The wet wood expanded, splitting off massive chunks of rock

4. **Making Correct Inferences**

   Two of the statements below are correct *inferences,* or reasonable guesses. They are based on information in the passage. The other statement is an incorrect, or faulty, inference. Label the statements C for *correct* inference and F for *faulty* inference.

   _____ a. The Egyptians could have completed the pyramids more quickly with blocks and tackles.

   _____ b. Backbreaking labor was required to build the pyramids.

   _____ c. The Egyptians accomplished marvels of engineering with primitive techniques.

5. **Understanding Main Ideas**

   One of the statements below expresses the main idea of the passage. One statement is too general, or too broad. The other explains only part of the passage; it is too narrow. Label the statements M for *main idea,* B for *too broad,* and N for *too narrow.*

   _____ a. The ancient Egyptians built the pyramids with simple copper and stone tools and muscle power.

   _____ b. Humans have been skilled at quarrying for many thousands of years.

   _____ c. The Egyptians used tools made of dolomite to quarry granite.

Correct Answers, Part A _____

Correct Answers, Part B _____

Total Correct Answers _____

Writers and Readers

The first step toward writing that communicates is to have something to say and to understand very clearly what it is. The second step is to understand the background and ability of the reader. The third step is to select the words that will effectively bridge the gap between the writer and the reader.

The three letters *d-o-g* form a word that children learn to read very early. The word refers to a common animal that they probably know well. If, however, a child lives in the far northern part of North America, the picture called up in the child's mind will probably be a husky pulling a sled over the snow. A child who lives in a large city may instead picture a small dog on a leash being taken for a walk on the street. A child who lives on a ranch might picture a large herding dog.

The meaning of a word therefore depends upon the experience of the reader—and the writer. If the writer of the word *dog* was thinking of a collie on a farm and the reader thinks of a lapdog on a leash, the beginning of a misunderstanding has taken place.

The type of dog brought to mind by the word *dog* is only one level of experience that can lead to misunderstanding between writer and reader. The group of experiences an individual has with something create a background of feelings and ideas associated with it. Perhaps as a child the writer was bitten by a dog. Later, as a teenager delivering pizzas, the writer was afraid to take a pizza to a house with a ferocious dog. Finally, as an adult, the writer might believe dogs are a nuisance. The word *dog* therefore calls up unpleasant experiences for the writer, which may be reflected in the writing. On the other hand, the reader may have had pleasant experiences with dogs; *dog* may be a favorable symbol.

Words thus have two kinds of meanings. Denotative meaning is relatively unchanging and refers to the thing the symbol stands for: the word *dog* means the animal known as a dog. Connotative meaning is the collective personal overtones suggested by the symbol. Both meanings depend upon the individual experiences of the writer and reader. No two people have exactly the same meaning for any word, because no two people have had exactly the same experience.

Reading Time _____

Recalling Facts

1. The first step toward writing that communicates is to
   - ❏ a. know the reader.
   - ❏ b. have something to say.
   - ❏ c. select the right words.

2. The meaning of a word depends upon
   - ❏ a. the area of the country where it is used.
   - ❏ b. the writer's and reader's experience.
   - ❏ c. the definition given in the dictionary.

3. Words have
   - ❏ a. one kind of meaning.
   - ❏ b. two kinds of meaning.
   - ❏ c. three kinds of meaning.

4. Denotative meaning
   - ❏ a. refers to the thing a symbol stands for.
   - ❏ b. is constantly changing.
   - ❏ c. reflects a mood.

5. Connotative meaning
   - ❏ a. can be found in a dictionary.
   - ❏ b. has personal overtones.
   - ❏ c. is the same for everyone.

Understanding Ideas

6. To a child who is afraid of water, the word *water* has a
   - ❏ a. denotative meaning.
   - ❏ b. negative connotation.
   - ❏ c. positive connotation.

7. The article suggests that the connotation of a word
   - ❏ a. can be both positive and negative.
   - ❏ b. is usually positive.
   - ❏ c. is either positive or negative.

8. You can conclude from the article that the definitions of words found in a dictionary give
   - ❏ a. connotative meanings.
   - ❏ b. denotative meanings.
   - ❏ c. both denotative and connotative meanings.

9. You can conclude from the article that word connotations
   - ❏ a. make communication more difficult.
   - ❏ b. help writers to be more precise.
   - ❏ c. are easily avoided.

10. Writers can help to bridge the gap between themselves and the reader by
    - ❏ a. avoiding the use of words with negative connotations.
    - ❏ b. writing clearly to avoid misunderstanding.
    - ❏ c. creating positive images.

Mrs. Malaprop

In 1775 the Irish playwright Richard Brinsley Sheridan wrote a play called *The Rivals.* Sheridan's plays, immensely popular on the London stage, were often hilarious.

For *The Rivals,* Sheridan created a character he named Mrs. Malaprop. He was fond of giving the characters in his plays names that suggested their character traits, and Mrs. Malaprop's name comes from the French word *malapropos,* which means "not appropriate."

Mrs. Malaprop used important-sounding words, but she used most of them incorrectly. For example, she used the word *analyzed* when she meant *paralyzed* and *pineapple* when she meant *pinnacle* (a high point).

Sheridan's play was a great hit. Soon everyone in London was laughing at Mrs. Malaprop and trying to catch one another in the kinds of mistakes she made with words. Because of Sheridan's character, a new word entered the English language. The word is *malapropism,* and it means a silly misuse of words that sound something alike.

Communication takes place because all speakers of a language have more or less the same understanding of what a word means. So when you use a fancy word, be sure you know its meaning. Don't take too much for granite.

1. Recognizing Words in Context

Find the word *hilarious* in the passage. One definition below is a *synonym* for that word; it means the same or almost the same thing. One definition is an *antonym;* it has the opposite or nearly opposite meaning. The other has a completely different meaning. Label the definitions S for *synonym,* A for *antonym,* and D for *different.*

_____ a. serious
_____ b. funny
_____ c. successful

2. Distinguishing Fact from Opinion

Two of the statements below present *facts,* which can be proved correct. The other statement is an *opinion,* which expresses someone's thoughts or beliefs. Label the statements F for *fact* and O for *opinion.*

_____ a. Richard Brinsley Sheridan was the author of *The Rivals.*
_____ b. Mrs. Malaprop is a character in Sheridan's play.
_____ c. The play was a great hit.

3. Keeping Events in Order

Label the statements below 1, 2, and 3 to show the order in which the events happened.

_____ a. People laughed at Mrs. Malaprop's mistakes.

_____ b. The word *malapropism* came to mean the silly misuse of words.

_____ c. Richard Sheridan created a character named Mrs. Malaprop.

4. Making Correct Inferences

Two of the statements below are correct *inferences,* or reasonable guesses. They are based on information in the passage. The other statement is an incorrect, or faulty, inference. Label the statements C for *correct* inference and F for *faulty* inference.

_____ a. The silly misuse of a word can be very funny.

_____ b. It is a mistake to use big words.

_____ c. Sheridan was a very clever playwright.

5. Understanding Main Ideas

One of the statements below expresses the main idea of the passage. One statement is too general, or too broad. The other explains only part of the passage; it is too narrow. Label the statements M for *main idea,* B for *too broad,* and N for *too narrow.*

_____ a. New words come into the language in different ways.

_____ b. Mrs. Malaprop, a character in Sheridan's play, used fancy words incorrectly, causing much laughter.

_____ c. The word *malapropism,* meaning the silly misuse of words, comes from the name of a character in a play—Mrs. Malaprop.

Correct Answers, Part A _____

Correct Answers, Part B _____

Total Correct Answers _____

The veneration and respect shown to the dead in many cultures and societies is known as ancestor worship. It is one of human history's oldest and most basic religious beliefs. Basic to this belief is the notion that when family members die, they join the spirit world and are closer to their god(s) than living people. These spirits, no longer burdened with bodies, are generally thought to be very powerful. Some believe such spirits possess the ability to help or to harm people in the living world and may even be powerful enough to be reborn into the community. The living who believe these things therefore view ancestors with a mixture of awe, fear, and respect. They feel dependent on the goodwill of their ancestors for prosperity and survival. Under such beliefs, the family link does not end with the physical death of the individual.

Those who practice ancestor worship often believe the dead have many of the same needs as they did when they were alive. Thus, the living believe in bestowing on them food and drink as well as respect, attention, and love. This veneration of ancestors may be carried out either by individuals or by the whole community. Community worship normally centers on a great leader or hero. Special days of the year are often set aside for such commemoration.

In some countries devotion to the ancestors and their needs is a part of everyday life. In China, for example, ancestor worship has long been a key religious belief and practice and ancient Chinese religious rituals that focus on ancestors continue today. The spirits of the ancestors are offered food, drink, incense, and prayers. They are asked to bless family events because they are still considered part of the family. Believers see no conflict in continuing to respect their own family saints while also revering other religious figures.

Ancestor worship is now thought to be a misleading term. *Ancestor respect* might be a more accurate term. This broadens the concept considerably but not illogically. Putting gifts and flowers on the graves of the family dead is probably the oldest universal human religious gesture and is an unmistakable sign of ancestor respect.

These practices, which are followed by members of modern societies as well as those who practice ancient cultural traditions, indicate a belief that at some level people continue to exist after they have died.

Reading Time _____

Recalling Facts

1. Ancestor worship is a belief that
   - ❏ a. humans become spirits after death.
   - ❏ b. physical death is the beginning of life.
   - ❏ c. death is the end of existence.

2. Veneration of ancestors often assumes that the dead
   - ❏ a. have many of the same needs as they did when they were alive.
   - ❏ b. are in conflict with the living.
   - ❏ c. lack physical bodies and never have physical needs.

3. Dead ancestors are considered
   - ❏ a. family leaders.
   - ❏ b. removed from the family.
   - ❏ c. part of the family.

4. Dead ancestors are revered because
   - ❏ a. they are thought to be closer to their god(s).
   - ❏ b. they are thought to be gods.
   - ❏ c. of the good deeds they performed while alive.

5. Devotion to ancestors often assumes that spirits are
   - ❏ a. ruthless.
   - ❏ b. powerful.
   - ❏ c. humorous.

Understanding Ideas

6. The term *ancestor respect* is replacing the term *ancestor worship* because
   - ❏ a. the term *worship* suggests a god.
   - ❏ b. worship can take place only in a church.
   - ❏ c. the living should not worship the dead.

7. Ancestors are often feared because of the belief that they
   - ❏ a. can control the success or failure of the living.
   - ❏ b. will be reborn into the community.
   - ❏ c. no longer have bodies.

8. For many cultures, the veneration of ancestors is
   - ❏ a. a misguided concept.
   - ❏ b. as basic a belief today as it was centuries ago.
   - ❏ c. a religious belief practiced mostly in China.

9. As with ancestor worship, a basic tenet of ancestor respect is that
   - ❏ a. heroic people should be venerated after they die.
   - ❏ b. humans exist as spirits after their physical death.
   - ❏ c. humans have no control over their lives.

10. You can conclude from the article that those who respect their ancestors
    - ❏ a. are primarily interested in their own well-being.
    - ❏ b. all have the same religious beliefs.
    - ❏ c. differ in their religious beliefs and practices.

Once a week my mother and I walk to the cemetery with food for my grandmother and other relatives who have died. We bring a little meat and bread, soup, and sometimes a jar of hot coffee to place near the graves.

First we clean the gravestones and the area all around them. We sweep off the soil the wind has blown over them, and we pull out weeds that have grown there. Then we sing the old honoring songs and memorial songs of our Lakota people. These songs have been passed down from person to person for many generations. My mother told me how her grandmother used to sing these songs whenever the soldiers came through our reservation. Everyone was proud of how brave she was!

In addition to placing food at our ancestors' graves, we honor the spirits of our ancestors at every main meal by setting a spirit plate for them. We take one plate, bless it, and fill it with a tiny bit of every food at the meal. Then we place the plate near the center of the table and pray over it before anyone eats. I never see anything disappear from the plate, but I know that the good spirits of my ancestors are eating the energy of the food. They know that they are remembered and celebrated.

1. **Recognizing Words in Context**

   Find the word *passed* in the passage. One definition below is a *synonym* for that word; it means the same or almost the same thing. One definition is an *antonym*; it has the opposite or nearly opposite meaning. The other has a completely different meaning. Label the definitions S for *synonym*, A for *antonym*, and D for *different*.

   _____ a. happened
   _____ b. transferred
   _____ c. withheld

2. **Distinguishing Fact from Opinion**

   Two of the statements below present *facts*, which can be proved correct. The other statement is an *opinion*, which expresses someone's thoughts or beliefs. Label the statements F for *fact* and O for *opinion*.

   _____ a. The narrator and the mother visit their ancestors' graves every week.
   _____ b. Before main meals, the family prepares a spirit plate for their ancestors.
   _____ c. The spirits eat the energy of the food on the spirit plate.

3. Keeping Events in Order

Two of the statements below describe events that happened at the same time. The other statement describes an event that happened before or after those events. Label them S for *same time,* B for *before,* or A for *after.*

_____ a. The mother's grandmother sang the honoring and memorial songs of her people.

_____ b. Soldiers came through the reservation.

_____ c. The mother and the narrator sang the honoring and memorial songs of their people.

4. Making Correct Inferences

Two of the statements below are correct *inferences,* or reasonable guesses. They are based on information in the passage. The other statement is an incorrect, or faulty, inference. Label the statements C for *correct* inference and F for *faulty* inference.

_____ a. The mother and the narrator respect their ancestors.

_____ b. Food plays an important role in the beliefs of the Lakota people.

_____ c. The mother and the narrator worship their ancestors.

5. Understanding Main Ideas

One of the statements below expresses the main idea of the passage. One statement is too general, or too broad. The other explains only part of the passage; it is too narrow. Label the statements M for *main idea,* B for *too broad,* and N for *too narrow.*

_____ a. The mother and the narrator honor their ancestors by providing food for them.

_____ b. The Lakota people show veneration and respect for the dead as do people of many other cultures.

_____ c. A spirit plate is blessed and filled with food.

Correct Answers, Part A _____

Correct Answers, Part B _____

Total Correct Answers _____

On a pier in New York Harbor in 1841 a crowd watched a ship from England being towed to the pier. There was no ocean communication cable as yet and the ship brought the latest news on a pressing question. The question was yelled from the pier to the ship: "Is Little Nell dead?" Little Nell was the heroine in a story called *The Old Curiosity Shop*. The latest installment of the serialized novel was on the ship, and the people were eager to learn how the story came out.

The author who could stir people to such excitement was Charles Dickens, then a young man of 29. With *The Pickwick Papers*, he had become the world's most celebrated writer.

Charles Dickens was born on February 7, 1812, in Portsmouth, England. His father, John Dickens, was a minor clerk in the navy offices. He was a friendly man with a large family and only a moderate income. Charles was the second of eight children. The family moved to London when Charles was 11 and after a series of financial disasters, John Dickens and his family ended up in a prison for debtors.

Young Charles was able to secure work in a blacking factory and lodging in a garret. On Sundays he visited his family in prison. When a timely inheritance restored the family to comfortable means, Charles had a few quiet years at a private school.

The qualities that made up Dickens's genius did not depend on formal education for development. His real education came from his reading and observation and daily experience. Dickens spent several years as a court reporter. He had a reporter's eye for the details of daily life and a mimic's ear for the subtleties of common speech. Further, he had the artist's ability to select what he needed from these raw materials of observation and to shape them into works of enduring merit. His novels all deal with his own day and environment, except for two historical novels, and reflect his concern for social justice and reform as well as a keen humor.

When his rising fortune and fame gave him control of a great newspaper, Dickens put his father on the staff to preside over the dispatches and bought him a small country house. He later immortalized his father as Mr. Micawber, a character in his most autobiographical novel, *The Personal History of David Copperfield*.

Reading Time _____

Recalling Facts

1. Charles Dickens became the world's most celebrated writer after
   - ❏ a. publishing a newspaper.
   - ❏ b. writing *The Pickwick Papers*.
   - ❏ c. serving time in prison.

2. Dickens lived during the
   - ❏ a. 17th century.
   - ❏ b. 18th century.
   - ❏ c. 19th century.

3. Dickens's family was placed in prison because
   - ❏ a. of unpaid debts.
   - ❏ b. his father was a spy.
   - ❏ c. of mistaken identity.

4. Life improved for the Dickens family after
   - ❏ a. Charles became wealthy.
   - ❏ b. they inherited money.
   - ❏ c. World War II.

5. Charles Dickens wrote about
   - ❏ a. daily life in America.
   - ❏ b. famous people.
   - ❏ c. life in England.

Understanding Ideas

6. Charles Dickens's writing fame was primarily the result of
   - ❏ a. a good education.
   - ❏ b. his ability to observe and write about daily experience.
   - ❏ c. his impoverished upbringing.

7. One reason people enjoyed reading Dickens's novels is that
   - ❏ a. he kept them in suspense.
   - ❏ b. they resembled English novels of the 18th century.
   - ❏ c. there were few novels published at the time.

8. It is likely that some of Dickens's characters were
   - ❏ a. based on people he knew.
   - ❏ b. famous people of the time.
   - ❏ c. people he met in prison.

9. You can conclude from the article that Charles Dickens's attitude toward his father was one of
   - ❏ a. hopelessness.
   - ❏ b. concern.
   - ❏ c. aversion.

10. You can conclude from the article that Charles Dickens preferred writing
   - ❏ a. books about history.
   - ❏ b. fiction.
   - ❏ c. news stories.

In 1842 Charles Dickens was one of the most popular writers in both England and the United States. At the age of 30 he had already published *The Pickwick Papers, Nicholas Nickleby,* and *The Old Curiosity Shop.* Edgar Allan Poe, at 32, was still not well known.

When Dickens arrived in Philadelphia on a lecture tour, Poe sent him a letter requesting a meeting. With his letter he enclosed a two-volume collection of his short stories. Dickens responded politely, and the two authors met twice in Dickens's hotel room.

The two men discussed English and American writers and other matters for a while. Finally, Poe got to the point. He wanted his book *Tales of the Grotesque and Arabesque* to be published in England. He asked Dickens to help him. Dickens promised that he would try. Nine months later, however, Dickens wrote to Poe telling him that he had failed: "I have mentioned it to publishers with whom I have influence, but they have, one and all, declined the venture."

Poe's biographer, Una Pope-Hennessy, later wrote that the meetings between Poe and Dickens "closed coldly. Neither seems to have liked the other much."

1. **Recognizing Words in Context**

   Find the word *closed* in the passage. One definition below is a *synonym* for that word; it means the same or almost the same thing. One definition is an *antonym;* it has the opposite or nearly opposite meaning. The other has a completely different meaning. Label the definitions S for *synonym,* A for *antonym,* and D for *different.*

   _____ a. started
   _____ b. ended
   _____ c. shut

2. **Distinguishing Fact from Opinion**

   Two of the statements below present *facts,* which can be proved correct. The other statement is an *opinion,* which expresses someone's thoughts or beliefs. Label the statements F for *fact* and O for *opinion.*

   _____ a. Charles Dickens was a popular writer, but Edgar Allan Poe was not well known.
   _____ b. Dickens and Poe met twice in 1842.
   _____ c. Dickens and Poe did not appear to like each other very much.

3. Keeping Events in Order

Two of the statements below describe events that happened at the same time. The other statement describes an event that happened before or after those events. Label them S for *same time*, B for *before*, or A for *after*.

_____ a. Poe sent Dickens a letter requesting a meeting.

_____ b. Poe asked Dickens to help him get a book published in England.

_____ c. Poe sent Dickens a collection of his short stories.

4. Making Correct Inferences

Two of the statements below are correct *inferences*, or reasonable guesses. They are based on information in the passage. The other statement is an incorrect, or faulty, inference. Label the statements C for *correct* inference and F for *faulty* inference.

_____ a. Because of Dickens's popularity, Poe thought he would be able to influence publishers.

_____ b. British publishers were not impressed with Poe's work.

_____ c. Because of his dislike for Poe, Dickens never really tried to get Poe's stories published in England.

5. Understanding Main Ideas

One of the statements below expresses the main idea of the passage. One statement is too general, or too broad. The other explains only part of the passage; it is too narrow. Label the statements M for *main idea*, B for *too broad*, and N for *too narrow*.

_____ a. Charles Dickens was one of the most popular writers of all time.

_____ b. In 1842 Edgar Allan Poe met with Charles Dickens in Philadelphia and asked Dickens for help publishing a book.

_____ c. Edgar Allan Poe was not as well known as Charles Dickens.

Correct Answers, Part A _____

Correct Answers, Part B _____

Total Correct Answers _____

Concrete is relatively cheap and durable and can be molded to any shape. It can be made porous or watertight, heavy or light, and will even harden under water. These and other variable characteristics of concrete make it ideal for many uses. Concrete building components are made in standard sizes and then put in place. They include wall panels, doorsills, beams, and floor slabs. Roads made of concrete are durable and can be maintained inexpensively.

To make concrete, appropriate amounts of dry ingredients are thoroughly blended together. Next, enough water is added to make a stiff but workable mixture. Concrete for home use in sidewalks, walls, and basement floors usually contains one part cement, two parts sand, and three parts stone or gravel. Blended, dry concrete ingredients can be purchased for home repairs and smaller projects and mixed as needed with water. Larger requirements are met by concrete mixed at the jobsite or by ready-mixed concrete, which is carried to the site in trucks. Concrete can also be mixed on its way to the jobsite by mixers that are mounted on trucks.

Properly mixed concrete does not pour. It is instead placed into mold-like forms that determine the shape the casting is to take. The forms may be made of lumber, plywood, reinforced plastics, or metal. They are first oiled or moistened to keep the hardened concrete from sticking to them. Shortly after the concrete is placed, a spade or other tool is worked up and down in it to remove trapped air. The concrete is then compacted by tamping the surface or by using mechanical vibrators.

Excess concrete is removed by screeding, or drawing a straightedge such as a board along the top of the form with a sawing motion. Smoothing, also called floating, and grading are accomplished by gently working the exposed concrete with a light metal, wood, or cork tool having a flat surface.

The ease with which concrete can be placed and worked depends on what is called its workability. Concrete that is too stiff is not workable. A very wet mixture pours and works easily but lacks strength. To improve workability while retaining strength, substances called plasticizers are sometimes added to concrete. Substances that create minute air bubbles also may be added to concrete, causing a slight loss of strength but increasing workability. Other additives are used to give concrete different characteristics to fit job requirements.

Reading Time _____

Recalling Facts

1. Concrete is made by mixing dry ingredients with
   - ❏ a. oil.
   - ❏ b. water.
   - ❏ c. gasoline.

2. Removing excess concrete is done by
   - ❏ a. scraping.
   - ❏ b. etching.
   - ❏ c. screeding.

3. The ease with which concrete can be placed and worked is called its
   - ❏ a. workability.
   - ❏ b. malleability.
   - ❏ c. durability.

4. Concrete is usually
   - ❏ a. poured.
   - ❏ b. placed into forms.
   - ❏ c. stacked in blocks.

5. Air bubbles added to concrete cause a loss of
   - ❏ a. workability.
   - ❏ b. shape.
   - ❏ c. strength.

Understanding Ideas

6. You can conclude from the article that concrete is made according to
   - ❏ a. a specific formula.
   - ❏ b. how it will be used.
   - ❏ c. where it is mixed.

7. The main factor influencing the workability of concrete is
   - ❏ a. the amount of water added to the dry mix.
   - ❏ b. the amount of concrete needed for the job.
   - ❏ c. air temperature.

8. Air trapped in concrete
   - ❏ a. increases its strength.
   - ❏ b. increases its workability.
   - ❏ c. must be removed.

9. Concrete is ideal for many uses because of its
   - ❏ a. strength.
   - ❏ b. low cost.
   - ❏ c. variable characteristics.

10. The biggest challenge in mixing concrete is to
    - ❏ a. improve workability while retaining strength.
    - ❏ b. make it as pourable as possible by using additives.
    - ❏ c. increase strength by decreasing workability.

A Short History of Cement

The ancient Romans were among the first to make and use cement. They mixed ground limestone and water with volcanic ash, a substance they had in copious supply after Etna, a Sicilian volcano, erupted. The ash created cement that hardened even under water. Roman cement was so strong that many of their cement roads, bridges, and buildings still survive centuries later.

When the Roman Empire fell around A.D. 400, however, the secret of making cement was lost. It was more than 1,300 years later, in 1756, when a British engineer, John Smaton, figured out how to make cement again. Once cement was rediscovered, chemists and engineers experimented with mixtures. The next big advance was Portland cement, a mixture of limestone and clay that was ground, baked, and reground. Invented in 1824, Portland cement was superior to natural cements because it did not crack or crumble as easily.

Meanwhile, builders were using cement to make concrete, a mixture of dry cement, water, sand, and gravel or stone that was cheaper, easier to make, and easier to work with than cement alone. By 1850 concrete reinforced with iron or steel bars came into use. This and other advances helped to make concrete one of the world's most popular construction materials.

1. Recognizing Words in Context

Find the word *copious* in the passage. One definition below is a *synonym* for that word; it means the same or almost the same thing. One definition is an *antonym;* it has the opposite or nearly opposite meaning. The other has a completely different meaning. Label the definitions S for *synonym,* A for *antonym,* and D for *different.*

_____ a. short
_____ b. plentiful
_____ c. manageable

2. Distinguishing Fact from Opinion

Two of the statements below present *facts,* which can be proved correct. The other statement is an *opinion,* which expresses someone's thoughts or beliefs. Label the statements F for *fact* and O for *opinion.*

_____ a. The Romans made and used cement.
_____ b. The secret of making cement was lost for 1,300 years.
_____ c. Portland cement is superior to natural cement.

3. Keeping Events in Order

Label the statements below 1, 2, and 3 to show the order in which the events happened.

_____ a. The Romans made and used cement.

_____ b. Portland cement was invented.

_____ c. John Smaton figured out how to make cement.

4. Making Correct Inferences

Two of the statements below are correct *inferences,* or reasonable guesses. They are based on information in the passage. The other statement is an incorrect, or faulty, inference. Label the statements C for *correct* inference and F for *faulty* inference.

_____ a. Cement has a long history as a construction material.

_____ b. No one has ever been able to make cement like the Romans.

_____ c. Cement remains an important material in modern construction.

5. Understanding Main Ideas

One of the statements below expresses the main idea of the passage. One statement is too general, or too broad. The other explains only part of the passage; it is too narrow. Label the statements M for *main idea,* B for *too broad,* and N for *too narrow.*

_____ a. Cement is an important building product.

_____ b. The secret of making cement, lost in A.D. 400, was not rediscovered until 1756.

_____ c. Cement, used in construction since Roman times, has undergone many advances through the centuries.

Correct Answers, Part A _____

Correct Answers, Part B _____

Total Correct Answers _____

The Alamo, an old fort in San Antonio, has been called the "Cradle of Texas Liberty." Its defense and the deaths of those who defended it inspired the cry, "Remember the Alamo!" Texas soldiers shouted this at the battle of San Jacinto, which brought Texas its independence from Mexico.

The Alamo was founded in 1718 by Spanish missionaries as the Mission San Antonio. By 1793 the mission church, later the famous fort, had fallen into disrepair and the mission was dissolved. At the time of its famous battle in 1836 the church was a roofless ruin. A high rock wall about three feet (one meter) thick enclosed an area around the church large enough to hold 1,000 men. Within that enclosure the battle of the Alamo was fought.

In December 1835 rebel Texans captured San Antonio in a significant battle. Most soldiers returned home to their families; only 80 soldiers were left to guard the city. More troops arrived later with orders to destroy the Alamo fortifications and move east with the artillery.

The Mexican commander Santa Anna was marching up through northern Mexico to regain the city. The commanding officer of the Alamo troops, Colonel William B. Travis, and Colonel James Bowie believed that the Alamo must be held to prevent Santa Anna's march into the Texas interior.

On February 22, 1836, the frontiersman Davy Crockett and 14 volunteer American riflemen arrived to help. On the same day, Santa Anna's force of almost 5,000 troops arrived. The next day, the Alamo forces and about 30 refugees withdrew into the fort and prepared for the Mexican attack. Santa Anna demanded unconditional surrender. A cannon shot from the fort came in reply. The Mexican bombardment followed.

On March 1, James Butler Bonham and a small group of volunteers arrived from nearby Gonzales to reinforce the Alamo troops. The defenders now numbered between 180 and 190.

The siege lasted 12 days. On the morning of March 6 several thousand Mexicans stormed the fort. Every Alamo defender died. Their bodies were burned at Santa Anna's order. The only survivors were 16 women and children. Nearly 1,600 Mexicans were killed. Six weeks later, General Sam Houston led the final battle at San Jacinto. Today the Alamo is preserved as a state park. In front of the old fort is a monument to those who died there. The battle call "Remember the Alamo!" honors these heroes.

Reading Time _____

Recalling Facts

1. The Alamo was built by
   - ❏ a. Texas soldiers.
   - ❏ b. Spanish missionaries.
   - ❏ c. Mexican workers.

2. The Alamo originally served as a
   - ❏ a. jail.
   - ❏ b. fort.
   - ❏ c. mission.

3. The siege at the Alamo took place during
   - ❏ a. the battle for Texas independence from Mexico.
   - ❏ b. the Spanish-American War.
   - ❏ c. World War I.

4. Mexican troops were led by
   - ❏ a. San Antonio.
   - ❏ b. Santa Anna.
   - ❏ c. San Jacinto.

5. "Remember the Alamo" was the battle call of
   - ❏ a. Mexican freedom fighters.
   - ❏ b. Alamo defenders.
   - ❏ c. soldiers at the battle of San Jacinto.

Understanding Ideas

6. At the time of the Alamo siege, the
   - ❏ a. Texans were greatly outnumbered.
   - ❏ b. Mexicans were greatly outnumbered.
   - ❏ c. Texans and Mexicans were evenly matched.

7. American volunteers helped to defend the Alamo, which suggests that
   - ❏ a. Americans believed in the cause of freedom.
   - ❏ b. Americans were hungry for battle.
   - ❏ c. Americans wanted Texas to belong to their country.

8. It is likely that soldiers inside the Alamo
   - ❏ a. thought that they would win the battle.
   - ❏ b. knew that they would be defeated.
   - ❏ c. planned to escape.

9. Calling the Alamo the "Cradle of Texas Liberty" means that
   - ❏ a. a baby was born there during the siege.
   - ❏ b. in death there is freedom.
   - ❏ c. the Alamo battle was the beginning of the Texans' fight for freedom.

10. The importance of the battle of the Alamo was that
    - ❏ a. Texas soldiers were defeated.
    - ❏ b. a battle was fought in a church institution.
    - ❏ c. it served to inspire soldiers fighting for Texas independence.

Davy Crockett was one of the heroes who fought and died defending the Alamo against Mexican forces in 1836. He had long been famous for his exploits as "king of the wild frontier." Crockett made sure of his fame when he published his "autobiography" in 1834. The book—tall tales that depicted Crockett as a larger-than-life hero—was a great success.

Even as a boy in Tennessee, Davy Crockett was better known for his exploits than for his interest in books. He didn't attend school until he was 13—and he stayed only four days. Following a fight at school, Davy ran away from home. He headed for Virginia with a cattle drover he met. There he joined up with a wagoner and traveled with him to Baltimore, Maryland. When the wagoner failed to pay him, Davy decided to return home. He was almost 16 when he arrived back in Tennessee. He had walked almost all the way!

During his travels, Davy changed his mind about education. He went back to school, where he learned enough to carry him through a career in politics. He served in the Tennessee legislature and in the United States Congress. When he was not reelected to Congress in 1835, he moved to Texas. There, at the Alamo, Davy Crockett became a legend.

1. **Recognizing Words in Context**

Find the word *failed* in the passage. One definition below is a *synonym* for that word; it means the same or almost the same thing. One definition is an *antonym*; it has the opposite or nearly opposite meaning. The other has a completely different meaning. Label the definitions S for *synonym*, A for *antonym*, and D for *different*.

_____ a. succeeded
_____ b. weakened
_____ c. neglected

2. **Distinguishing Fact from Opinion**

Two of the statements below present *facts*, which can be proved correct. The other statement is an *opinion*, which expresses someone's thoughts or beliefs. Label the statements F for *fact* and O for *opinion*.

_____ a. Davy Crockett died fighting at the Alamo.
_____ b. Davy Crockett was a larger-than-life hero.
_____ c. Davy Crockett served in the United States Congress.

3. Keeping Events in Order

Label the statements below 1, 2, and 3 to show the order in which the events happened.

_____ a. Davy Crockett was not reelected to Congress.

_____ b. Davy Crockett died fighting at the Alamo.

_____ c. Davy Crockett moved to Texas.

4. Making Correct Inferences

Two of the statements below are correct *inferences*, or reasonable guesses. They are based on information in the passage. The other statement is an incorrect, or faulty, inference. Label the statements C for *correct* inference and F for *faulty* inference.

_____ a. Without education, Davy Crockett could not have had a career in politics.

_____ b. Davy Crockett was a popular hero of his time.

_____ c. Davy Crockett was willing to give his life for his beliefs.

5. Understanding Main Ideas

One of the statements below expresses the main idea of the passage. One statement is too general, or too broad. The other explains only part of the passage; it is too narrow. Label the statements M for *main idea*, B for *too broad*, and N for *too narrow*.

_____ a. Davy Crockett, one of the heroes of the Alamo, was known for his lifelong exploits.

_____ b. Davy Crockett ran away from home at the age of 13.

_____ c. Davy Crockett was just one of many heroes who died in the battle of the Alamo.

Correct Answers, Part A _____

Correct Answers, Part B _____

Total Correct Answers _____

Dry Cleaning Isn't Dry

Garments and other articles that are washed in liquids other than water are said to be dry-cleaned. Certain fabrics cannot stand up under regular laundering and must be cleaned in this way. The dry-cleaning process is not actually dry. It is called dry because water is not used. Most modern dry-cleaning fluids are either petroleum or synthetic solvents. Different equipment is required for each of the solvents. Petroleum types can be used in open washing machines. Synthetic solvents evaporate very quickly in the air. They are used in closed, airtight washing machines.

In the dry-cleaning plant, garments and other items are first labeled with a mark or tag. Usually fabrics are examined to see if there are any badly worn or faulty parts. These might not survive the dry-cleaning process without further damage. Such areas cannot always be found by a visual inspection. Many items are measured before cleaning if the material is thought to be shrinkable. The measurements are marked on the identification tag for the guidance of the finishers.

Items for cleaning are next classified and sorted into separate portable hampers according to their fibers. Wool, silk and rayon, cotton and linen, and synthetic fibers are some of the most common classifications. The items then are further separated by colors—dark, medium, and light. Garments make up the bulk of articles that are dry-cleaned. Draperies and fine table-cloths are often dry-cleaned also.

After the articles have been sorted, they are agitated in a clear solvent and then in a soapy solvent. Next they are rinsed in a clear solution. A dry-cleaning machine using petroleum solvent contains a perforated metal cylinder, which revolves slowly in a metal shell containing the cleaning substance. The synthetic-solvent machine is sealed airtight and the cleaning fluid is then pumped into it.

Next the items are placed in an extractor. Here centrifugal force removes most of the moisture. If a petroleum solvent is used, the garments are then placed either in a drying tumbler or a drying cabinet. The tumbler consists of a rotating woven wire cylinder supported and housed within a metal casing. In addition to drying the solvent, it also deodorizes it.

The drying cabinet is used for items that cannot withstand rotary drying action, such as silk or rayon clothing. The cabinet must be properly ventilated to remove solvent gases or moisture. This is done by changing the air every few minutes.

Reading Time _____

Recalling Facts

1. The dry-cleaning process is called dry because
   - ❏ a. it is actually dry.
   - ❏ b. no water is used.
   - ❏ c. no fluids are used.

2. Modern dry-cleaning fluids include synthetic solvents and
   - ❏ a. gasoline.
   - ❏ b. bleach.
   - ❏ c. petroleum.

3. Items to be dry-cleaned are first separated according to
   - ❏ a. size.
   - ❏ b. fibers.
   - ❏ c. weight.

4. If the material is thought to be shrinkable, an item is
   - ❏ a. not able to be dry-cleaned.
   - ❏ b. measured before it is cleaned.
   - ❏ c. stretched after it is cleaned.

5. Most items cleaned are
   - ❏ a. garments.
   - ❏ b. draperies.
   - ❏ c. bed linens.

Understanding Ideas

6. You can conclude from the article that items that must be dry-cleaned
   - ❏ a. would be damaged by laundering with water.
   - ❏ b. are mostly synthetic.
   - ❏ c. can also be laundered with water.

7. It is likely that items are sorted by colors before cleaning
   - ❏ a. to prevent colors from running during the cleaning process.
   - ❏ b. to make separation after cleaning easier.
   - ❏ c. so that drying time is shortened.

8. You can conclude from the article that dry cleaning is
   - ❏ a. a relatively simple process.
   - ❏ b. a complicated process.
   - ❏ c. the most inexpensive cleaning process.

9. You can conclude from the article that rotary drying action is appropriate for
   - ❏ a. all kinds of fabrics.
   - ❏ b. delicate fabrics.
   - ❏ c. durable fabrics.

10. You can conclude from the article that solvent gases resulting from dry cleaning
    - ❏ a. are harmful to fabrics.
    - ❏ b. should not be inhaled by humans.
    - ❏ c. can be reused.

Wash Day

"Wake up, Gerda! It's wash day." Mother's voice stirred Gerda from a pleasant dream. Wash day! How she hated it.

Gerda hauled pailful after pailful of water from the well to fill the huge pot hanging from a tripod over a fire. Gerda next carried armloads of soiled clothing and sheets and pushed them down into the water with a wooden paddle. Taking a bar of homemade lye soap, Gerda rubbed the soap into the soaked clothes. The harsh lye reddened her skin and stung her eyes.

Gerda stood on a box next to the pot and turned the paddle round and round, stirring the clothes in the hot water. Her mother used another paddle to pull out the dripping clothes one by one. Working together, they wrung the water out of the clothes and placed them on the grass. She and Gerda tipped the hot, soapy water out of the pot. Then Gerda had to haul more pailfuls of clean water to rinse the clothes in.

Later, as Gerda wearily helped hang the clean clothing on lines strung between poles, she thought, "Maybe someone will come up with a better way of cleaning clothes someday."

1. **Recognizing Words in Context**

   Find the word *soiled* in the passage. One definition below is a *synonym* for that word; it means the same or almost the same thing. One definition is an *antonym;* it has the opposite or nearly opposite meaning. The other has a completely different meaning. Label the definitions S for *synonym*, A for *antonym,* and D for *different*.

   _____ a. corrupted
   _____ b. dirty
   _____ c. clean

2. **Distinguishing Fact from Opinion**

   Two of the statements below present *facts,* which can be proved correct. The other statement is an *opinion,* which expresses someone's thoughts or beliefs. Label the statements F for *fact* and O for *opinion.*

   _____ a. Gerda hated wash day.
   _____ b. Gerda hauled pailfuls of water to fill the pot.
   _____ c. Gerda stirred the clothes with a paddle.

3. Keeping Events in Order

Label the statements below 1, 2, and 3 to show the order in which the events happened.

_____ a. Gerda pushed the clothes into the water with a paddle.

_____ b. Gerda stirred the clothes round and round with the paddle.

_____ c. Gerda rubbed lye soap into the clothes.

4. Making Correct Inferences

Two of the statements below are correct *inferences*, or reasonable guesses. They are based on information in the passage. The other statement is an incorrect, or faulty, inference. Label the statements C for *correct* inference and F for *faulty* inference.

_____ a. This story takes place before automatic washing machines existed.

_____ b. Clothes were not washed on a daily basis.

_____ c. Gerda and her mother were too poor to afford a washing machine.

5. Understanding Main Ideas

One of the statements below expresses the main idea of the passage. One statement is too general, or too broad. The other explains only part of the passage; it is too narrow. Label the statements M for *main idea*, B for *too broad*, and N for *too narrow*.

_____ a. Gerda hated the hard work of washing clothes and wished there were a better way to do it.

_____ b. Gerda rubbed the clothes with homemade lye soap.

_____ c. Since ancient times, people have had to find ways to clean their clothes.

Correct Answers, Part A _____

Correct Answers, Part B _____

Total Correct Answers _____

Long before people began to culture fishes, they were harvesting wild fishes from streams, lakes, and the oceans. As hunters began to domesticate land animals and others learned to plant agricultural crops, ancient fishers captured and raised wild fishes. The Chinese raised fishes as early as the 5th century B.C. The ancient Greeks cultured oysters in Rome and Gaul.

Aquaculture is a broad term that includes the culture of fishes, mollusks, crustaceans, algae, and even bullfrogs and alligators. Fish culture is the process of raising desirable species of fishes in captivity and managing them and their environment to improve growth and reproduction. Fishes are reared in fish farms, or hatcheries, much as farm animals are raised in the barnyard. The fish culturist manages the aquatic environment to protect the fishes from predators, parasites, and disease. The culturist also feeds the fishes and controls water quality to prevent pollution.

In the United States many fishes are raised in hatcheries and released in streams, rivers, and lakes to provide sport fishing. Fishes that live in the sea but return to fresh water to spawn, such as salmon, are released into rivers to swim to the ocean. When these fishes mature, they instinctively return to the river from which they were released. Small fishes such as minnows and goldfish are raised and sold for bait. Freshwater and saltwater forms of tropical fishes are raised and sold as aquarium fishes. On a world scale, most fishes that are reared by fish culturists are intended to provide food for humans.

Fishes may be cultured in tanks, ponds, nets, pens, or raceways—long, narrow channels with flowing water. Trout and salmon, which live in cold water, are cultured in raceways or in large round tanks and floating cages or pens. Culture of coldwater fishes is limited to hatchery sites with clean, cold water. Most coldwater fishes cannot live in contaminated water.

Channel catfish, common carp, and panfish such as bluegills, sunfishes, and bass are some of the warmwater fishes that are raised for food and sport, mostly in earthen ponds. Hatchery ponds may be as small as 1/10 acre (.04 hectares) or less, whereas commercial catfish ponds may be 20 acres (8 hectares) or more. Some catfish farms are so large that the fish are fed from aircraft. On some of these farms, the fish may eat 20 tons (20.4 tonnes) of feed in one day.

Reading Time _____

Recalling Facts

1. Raising fishes and managing their environment is called
   - ❏ a. channeling.
   - ❏ b. aquaculture.
   - ❏ c. hatching.

2. Coldwater fishes are very sensitive to
   - ❏ a. sunlight.
   - ❏ b. water pollution.
   - ❏ c. parasites.

3. Ancient Greeks cultured
   - ❏ a. oysters.
   - ❏ b. wild animals.
   - ❏ c. crabs.

4. Fishes that live in the sea but return to fresh water to spawn include
   - ❏ a. clams.
   - ❏ b. goldfish.
   - ❏ c. salmon.

5. Most fishes reared by fish culturists are sold as
   - ❏ a. aquarium fishes.
   - ❏ b. food for humans.
   - ❏ c. bait.

Understanding Ideas

6. The number of catfish raised commercially suggests that catfish
   - ❏ a. are popular food fish.
   - ❏ b. are not edible.
   - ❏ c. eat more than other fish.

7. You can conclude from the article that salmon raised in hatcheries are released into rivers in order to
   - ❏ a. prolong their lives.
   - ❏ b. increase the sport fish population.
   - ❏ c. restore the balance of nature.

8. It is likely that compared to fishes in the wild, cultured fishes
   - ❏ a. grow larger.
   - ❏ b. are more apt to die from disease.
   - ❏ c. eat less.

9. You can conclude from the article that compared to coldwater fish, warmwater fish are
   - ❏ a. more sensitive to pollution.
   - ❏ b. less sensitive to pollution.
   - ❏ c. not sensitive to pollution.

10. You can conclude from the article that fish farming is
    - ❏ a. a 20th century concept.
    - ❏ b. an ancient concept.
    - ❏ c. limited to the United States.

Fish was one of the favorite foods of Licinius Murena. "I wish I could have fresh fish available at all times," he said to himself one day. A wealthy Roman, Licinius soon found a way to satisfy his craving. He had huge fish tanks constructed on his estate. To supply the tanks with fresh seawater, Licinius spent a fortune having a channel dug from the ocean. As he gazed at the fish swarming in his tanks, Licinius smiled at the thought of endless fish dinners.

Mullet was a special favorite of Licinius's. To assure a supply of breeding stock, Licinius had workers tie fishing lines to the gills of male mullet and release the fish into the sea. After a while, the fish were reeled in back to the farm—followed by interested female mullet. During the season when mullet laid their eggs, the opposite method was used: female mullet tied to lines were sent to sea to bring in male mullet.

As Licinius displayed his fish farm to his friends, he pointed out his attempts at creating a natural environment for his fish. "Note the seaweed-covered rocks in the pools," he remarked. "Though they are prisoners, the fish will feel their captivity as little as possible."

1. Recognizing Words in Context

Find the word *natural* in the passage. One definition below is a *synonym* for that word; it means the same or almost the same thing. One definition is an *antonym;* it has the opposite or nearly opposite meaning. The other has a completely different meaning. Label the definitions S for *synonym,* A for *antonym,* and D for *different.*

_____ a. realistic
_____ b. artificial
_____ c. inborn

2. Distinguishing Fact from Opinion

Two of the statements below present *facts,* which can be proved correct. The other statement is an *opinion,* which expresses someone's thoughts or beliefs. Label the statements F for *fact* and O for *opinion.*

_____ a. Male mullet were used to lure female mullet from the sea.

_____ b. There is no better food than fresh fish.

_____ c. Licinius had a channel dug to bring water from the sea to his fish tanks.

3. Keeping Events in Order

Label the statements below 1, 2, and 3 to show the order in which the events happened.

_____ a. Licinius had huge fish tanks constructed on his estate.

_____ b. Licinius had a channel dug to bring water from the sea.

_____ c. Licinius Murena wanted fresh fish at all times.

4. Making Correct Inferences

Two of the statements below are correct *inferences*, or reasonable guesses. They are based on information in the passage. The other statement is an incorrect, or faulty, inference. Label the statements C for *correct* inference and F for *faulty* inference.

_____ a. Murena's friends also wanted to build fish farms.

_____ b. Creating a fish farm required a lot of money.

_____ c. Licinius Murena was willing to spend a great deal to satisfy his desire for fresh fish.

5. Understanding Main Ideas

One of the statements below expresses the main idea of the passage. One statement is too general, or too broad. The other explains only part of the passage; it is too narrow. Label the statements M for *main idea*, B for *too broad*, and N for *too narrow*.

_____ a. Licinius Murena tried to provide a natural environment for the fish in his tanks.

_____ b. Fish have been farmed throughout the world since ancient times.

_____ c. Licinius Murena, a wealthy Roman, created a fish farm on his estate.

Correct Answers, Part A _____

Correct Answers, Part B _____

Total Correct Answers _____

ANSWER KEY

READING RATE GRAPH

COMPREHENSION SCORE GRAPH

COMPREHENSION SKILLS PROFILE GRAPH

ANSWER KEY

1A	1. b	2. b	3. b	4. a	5. c	6. a	7. c	8. a	9. b	10. b
1B	1. D, S, A		2. F, O, F		3. 3, 2, 1		4. F, C, C		5. N, M, B	
2A	1. b	2. c	3. c	4. a	5. b	6. a	7. a	8. b	9. b	10. a
2B	1. S, D, A		2. O, F, F		3. 3, 2, 1		4. C, F, C		5. M, N, B	
3A	1. b	2. a	3. b	4. a	5. c	6. b	7. a	8. a	9. b	10. a
3B	1. S, A, D		2. F, O, F		3. 3, 2, 1		4. F, C, C		5. N, M, B	
4A	1. a	2. b	3. c	4. a	5. c	6. b	7. b	8. b	9. a	10. a
4B	1. D, S, A		2. F, F, O		3. 1, 3, 2		4. C, F, C		5. M, B, N	
5A	1. c	2. a	3. c	4. a	5. a	6. a	7. b	8. b	9. b	10. b
5B	1. A, S, D		2. F, F, O		3. 2, 3, 1		4. C, F, C		5. B, N, M	
6A	1. c	2. b	3. a	4. b	5. c	6. c	7. b	8. a	9. a	10. b
6B	1. A, S, D		2. F, F, O		3. 1, 2, 3		4. C, F, C		5. B, N, M	
7A	1. b	2. c	3. c	4. b	5. b	6. c	7. b	8. a	9. b	10. c
7B	1. S, A, D		2. F, F, O		3. 1, 3, 2		4. C, F, C		5. N, B, M	
8A	1. c	2. a	3. b	4. b	5. c	6. c	7. a	8. b	9. b	10. b
8B	1. D, A, S		2. F, F, O		3. 2, 1, 3		4. F, C, C		5. M, N, B	
9A	1. b	2. c	3. b	4. b	5. c	6. a	7. a	8. c	9. b	10. a
9B	1. D, S, A		2. F, F, O		3. B, S, S		4. F, C, C		5. N, B, M	
10A	1. b	2. c	3. a	4. c	5. b	6. c	7. a	8. a	9. b	10. a
10B	1. A, S, D		2. F, F, O		3. 2, 3, 1		4. C, F, C		5. B, N, M	
11A	1. a	2. c	3. b	4. b	5. b	6. b	7. b	8. a	9. c	10. c
11B	1. D, A, S		2. F, F, O		3. B, S, S		4. C, F, C		5. N, B, M	
12A	1. c	2. c	3. b	4. b	5. b	6. a	7. b	8. b	9. b	10. a
12B	1. S, D, A		2. O, F, F		3. 3, 2, 1		4. C, F, C		5. B, N, M	
13A	1. b	2. c	3. a	4. a	5. c	6. b	7. c	8. c	9. b	10. b
13B	1. A, S, D		2. O, F, F		3. A, S, S		4. C, C, F		5. M, B, N	

14A	1. b	2. c	3. b	4. a	5. c	6. c	7. b	8. a	9. a	10. a
14B	1. A, D, S	2. F, O, F	3. 1, 3, 2	4. C, C, F	5. B, M, N					
15A	1. c	2. b	3. b	4. c	5. a	6. b	7. a	8. a	9. a	10. b
15B	1. A, D, S	2. F, F, O	3. 2, 1, 3	4. C, F, C	5. B, N, M					
16A	1. b	2. b	3. c	4. c	5. c	6. c	7. b	8. a	9. a	10. b
16B	1. D, S, A	2. F, O, F	3. S, B, S	4. C, C, F	5. N, M, B					
17A	1. b	2. c	3. c	4. b	5. c	6. b	7. b	8. a	9. a	10. a
17B	1. S, D, A	2. O, F, F	3. B, S, S	4. C, F, C	5. M, N, B					
18A	1. b	2. a	3. b	4. c	5. c	6. c	7. a	8. a	9. c	10. a
18B	1. A, S, D	2. O, F, F	3. 2, 1, 3	4. F, C, C	5. M, B, N					
19A	1. b	2. b	3. b	4. a	5. b	6. b	7. a	8. b	9. a	10. b
19B	1. A, S, D	2. F, F, O	3. 2, 3, 1	4. C, F, C	5. B, N, M					
20A	1. a	2. a	3. c	4. a	5. b	6. a	7. a	8. b	9. b	10. c
20B	1. D, S, A	2. F, F, O	3. S, S, A	4. C, C, F	5. M, B, N					
21A	1. b	2. c	3. a	4. b	5. c	6. b	7. a	8. a	9. b	10. b
21B	1. A, S, D	2. F, F, O	3. S, A, S	4. C, C, F	5. B, M, N					
22A	1. b	2. c	3. a	4. b	5. c	6. b	7. a	8. c	9. c	10. a
22B	1. A, S, D	2. F, F, O	3. 1, 3, 2	4. C, F, C	5. B, N, M					
23A	1. b	2. c	3. a	4. b	5. c	6. a	7. a	8. b	9. c	10. c
23B	1. A, D, S	2. F, O, F	3. 1, 3, 2	4. F, C, C	5. M, N, B					
24A	1. b	2. c	3. b	4. b	5. a	6. a	7. a	8. b	9. c	10. b
24B	1. D, S, A	2. O, F, F	3. 1, 3, 2	4. C, C, F	5. M, N, B					
25A	1. b	2. b	3. a	4. c	5. b	6. a	7. b	8. a	9. b	10. b
25B	1. S, A, D	2. F, O, F	3. 2, 3, 1	4. F, C, C	5. N, B, M					

READING RATE

Put an X on the line above each lesson number to show your reading time and words-per-minute rate for that unit.

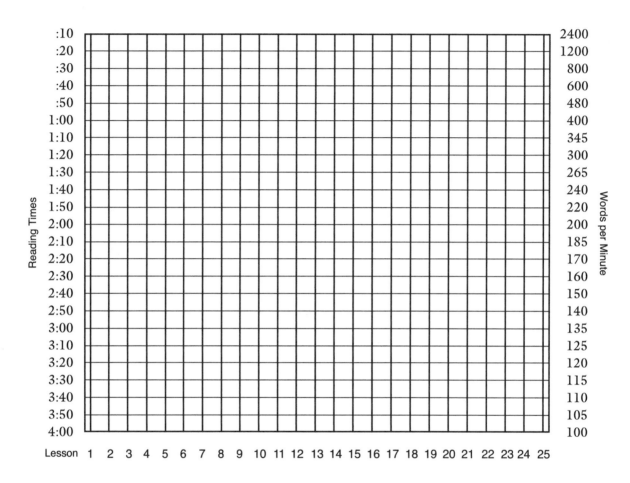

COMPREHENSION SCORE

Put an X on the line above each lesson number to indicate your total correct answers and comprehension score for that unit.

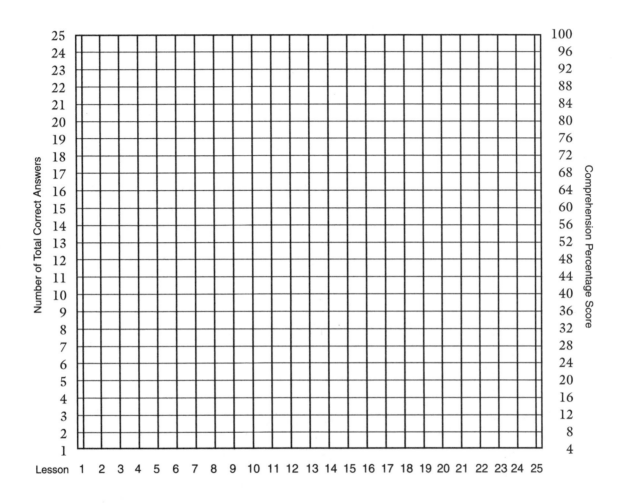

Comprehension Skills Profile

Put an X in the box above each question type to indicate an incorrect reponse to any part of that question.

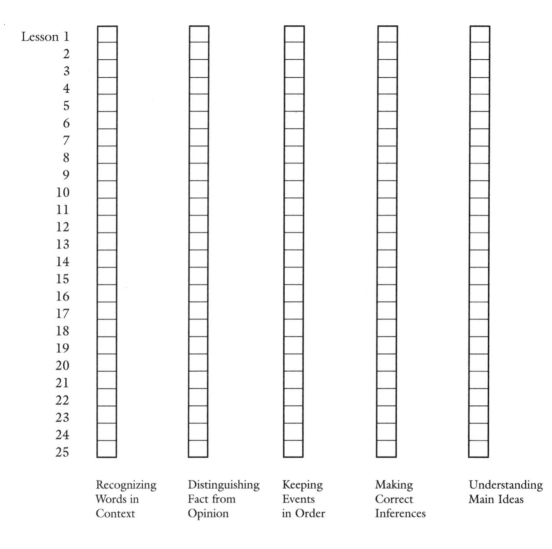

Lesson 1					
2					
3					
4					
5					
6					
7					
8					
9					
10					
11					
12					
13					
14					
15					
16					
17					
18					
19					
20					
21					
22					
23					
24					
25					

| Recognizing Words in Context | Distinguishing Fact from Opinion | Keeping Events in Order | Making Correct Inferences | Understanding Main Ideas |